POLICING IN A DIVIDED SOCIETY

FIGHTING A DIVIDED SOCIETY

Policing in a Divided Society

A study of part time policing in Northern Ireland

RICHARD MAPSTONE
Faculty of Business and Management
University of Ulster at Jordanstown

Avebury

Aldershot · Brookfield USA · Hong Kong · Singapore · Sydney

Published by
Avebury
Ashgate Publishing Limited
Gower House
Croft Road
Aldershot
Hants GU11 3HR
England

Ashgate Publishing Company
Old Post Road
Brookfield
Vermont 05036
USA

British Library Cataloguing in Publication Data

Mapstone, Richard H.
    Policing in a Divided Society: Study of Part Time Policing
    in Northern Ireland
    I. Title
    363.209416
 ISBN 1 85628 598 7

Library of Congress Cataloging-in-Publication Data

Mapstone, Richard H.
    Policing in a divided society: a study of part time policing in
    Northern Ireland / Richard Mapstone
       p. cm.
    Includes bibliographical references.
    ISBN 1-85628-598-7 : $59.95 (approx.)
    1. Royal Ulster Constabulary. 2. Constables--Ulster (Northern Ireland
    and Ireland) 3. Auxilary police--Ulster (Northern Ireland and Ireland)
    I. Title
    HV8197.5.A45R686 1994
    363.2'09416--dc20
                                          94-15829
                                               CIP

Printed and Bound in Great Britain by
Athenaeum Press Ltd, Newcastle upon Tyne.

Contents

Figures and tables

Acknowledgements

There are many people whose assistance was crucial to the developmennt of this study. I should therefore like to express my appreciation to all those who have contributed knowingly and unknowingly to the development of this book. In particular I would like to thank Sir John Herman former chief constable of the RUC for permission to carry out this study.

Many of those whose assistance I sought cannot be named fully for security reasons. However I should like to record my gratitude to Paddy, for his assistance at the initial stages of my work. I would also like to thank Cecil, my RUC liaison officer, and Ivan, and the staff of the RUC reserve office for their great friendliness patience and support. None of these officers of course bears any responsibility for the conclusions and observations made in this study.

The book would not have been possible without the assistance of members of the part time RUC reserve. Their dedication and commitment left a deep and lasting impression upon me. Unfortunately I cannot mention any of these officers by name but I thank them all for their unstinting help and enthusiasm.

Finally I would thank the University of Ulster and members of staff of the Human Resource Management group at the university. These colleagues gave me the time to carry out the study and tolerated my prolonged absences. I would also thank members of the administrative staff at the university who transcribed my tapes and typed my work.

Preface

Northern Ireland is a society which since its creation has been inflamed by deep religious and political divisions. These divisions have divided communities and nurtured an active terrorist campaign lasting many generations.

The idea for a book of this kind was developed during the early stages of a wider research project on which I was engaged which looked at the indigenous security forces in Northern Ireland. This book offers an analysis of the attitudes of part time members of the Royal Ulster Constabulary Reserve all of whom, at the end of a day's work, spend many extra hours a week on paid policing duties.

The book explores the reasons why people give up their spare time to share the hazards of fighting to preserve peace in the face of a terrorist campaign. In particular, the book looks at how part time police men and women, living and working in society fulfil the tasks of policing divided communities.

The part time RUC reserve has a planned strength of 2,000 members and represent a significant element of the overall composition of the police in Northern Ireland. This exploration of the part time police uses the language of the reservists themselves to explore their family and social backgrounds, their attitudes towards policing and toward the range of social and political issues that currently confront Northern Ireland.

The book is written at a time when there is a new and developing search for peace within the province, inspired by the Westminster/Dublin accord on the future of the province which was signed at the close of 1993. This new debate may reflect a developing pan Irish republican consensus and growing anxiety on the part of many in the protestant community, who may feel themselves confused and marginalized in this debate. The book is written against a backcloth of emerging protestant paramilitary violence. Since 1991 protestant paramilitary violence has outstripped the violent republican campaign in Northern Ireland.

It is self evident that we are all part of the society in which we live. In undertaking this research therefore I cannot claim a detachment from the issues that remain central to this society. These are issues that are fundamental to the structure of society and upon which few in Northern Ireland can remain neutral. My commitment to the RUC therefore dominates the perspective of this book. I was impressed by the dedication and commitment of part time police officers, who were often the unsung heroes of the force. Indeed the issues of policing in the province and the attitudes of police men and women, may prove of critical importance as the search for peace progresses. This book therefore offers a unique insight into these views. It identifies a number of important issues that should be addressed by the RUC if it is to move forward toward a model of impartial and professional policing.

1 An introduction to the study

Introduction

A central concern of this book is to identify the nature of the explanations members of the RUC reserve provide for their membership of the police and their behaviour within it. These explanations vary not simply because the officers exhibit different attitudes toward policing, but because they bring different backgrounds and expectations to their membership of the RUC reserve, which derive from the multiple statuses and relationships that they hold outside of the force. The social meanings attached to part time policing in Northern Ireland depend therefore upon the officers' backgrounds and knowledge of everyday routines and social encounters. It is therefore critical to understand the nature of the relationship between the RUC reservist and the wider community, and the manner in which the community supports the reserve. The book highlights the considerable variations that exist in the attitudes and values of part time members of the reserve. It represents the first comprehensive empirical study of the views of an important element of the RUC.

Part time members of a police force are in a unique position. As part time workers, their identification with the prevailing full time occupational culture may well be lessened by the shorter time during which they are exposed to it, and by their possession of another occupational role. They are essentially marginal to the main workforce. The process of establishing shared values and beliefs in their police work between themselves and their full time colleagues is therefore constrained by their limited involvement within the organization. As part time officers they may also be relatively isolated from the mainstream of police activity, and they may as a consequence be regarded with some hostility by full time officers as not being fully fledged members of the force, perhaps as less committed or more amateur.

It is important to identify at the outset some of the basic features of the society within which the RUC recruit and operate. These features distinguish the uniqueness of Northern Irish society in contrast to the social structures prevalent in the rest of the United Kingdom or Ireland and suggest a particular set of influences which mould and create its institutions.

Northern Irish society

A study of Northern Ireland society is primarily a study of social boundaries epitomized by internal division of society into protestant and catholic. Religion subsumes other identities; it is ascribed at birth, and determines social membership, and structures the pattern of interaction between individuals. The nature of an individual's locality, and often the individuals' place of work, politics, education and national identity thus become in this society codetermined with religion. It is true that the labels protestant and catholic are broad indicators, and underplay the political and social complexities within each category. They are however an important shorthand for describing patterns of social and cultural allegiance which constitute social divisions and reinforce mutual ignorance and hostility between the catholic minority community which predominantly subscribes to an all Ireland nationalist aspiration, and the protestant majority often described as "unionist" since it broadly supports the union of Northern Ireland with the rest of the United Kingdom.

Elliot and Hickie (1972) suggest that in Northern Ireland both communities are particularly concerned to avoid kinship interactions with "the other side". The more personal the interaction the more it is resisted. Endogamous marriage has been a traditional feature of Northern Ireland society. Language is also used to reinforce and preserve the boundaries between communities. The confining nature of interaction to "one's own kind" implies that communication rests on shared experiences and understandings.

Membership of a particular community ascribes therefore a basic status within society. Northern Irish society is characterized by a unity of personal relationships, where "community" dominates the structure of these relationships. To this extent we can talk of Northern Ireland as displaying many aspects of what Tonnies (1971) refers to as *Gemeinschaft* society where the traditional nature of the society is characterized by particularistic and ascribed relations. Within Northern Ireland relationships are personalized, individuals relating to each other not simply in terms of immediate transactions but rather in terms of the totality of their experience of each other. Individuals mediate their personal relationships by severe limiting of the frequency and type of interaction. *Gemeinschaft* society suggests that social life and work activity are patterned along lines of personal relationships. In Northern Ireland, it is suggested that such personal relationships are mediated by the religious allegiance ascribed at birth. Action is a symbolic derivation conducted according to a limited range of consensual norms which are shared and understood by the actors.

The type of society here described affects the development of institutions. *Gesellschaft* societies, where class or status divisions dominate, can expect clear distinctions to exist between the spheres of work, family and education. They operate as distinct realms of separate activity, each with separate recruitment paths. In Northern Ireland the traditional nature of the community structure suggests that social life and social activity are patterned along the fault lines created by religion. The spheres of work, family and education thus lack clear distinction. Recruitment to work and leisure activity has traditionally taken place on the basis of initial religious identity. Each community holds and maintains a range of institutional labels which act as community identifiers locating the individual within a particular group. Institutions may thus perform the interrelated roles of being both identified with a particular community and also symbols of community allegiance.

There exists therefore strong community "ideologies". These contain systematic assertions about Northern Ireland and the distribution of power in society. Such community ideologies derive in part from accumulated historical contingencies and create in the society a "crisis of authority". This occurs because it is within the protestant community that adherence to the structure of law and order is implicit in the community's value structure.

This type of social structure may result in what Manning and Butler (1982) describe as a "traditionalist" model of policing. Within this traditional model, social control is based upon community compliance with local values and preferences. Within Northern Ireland, the policing of unionist values features both as the basis of social order and provides a meaning system which acts to confirm the community and the position of the police within it. At the heart of this social division therefore lies the authority and status of the state and its laws. These features distinguish the uniqueness of Northern Irish society from the rest of the United Kingdom or indeed the rest of Ireland. It suggests a particular set of influences which have moulded and created its institutions.

3

It would be naive to assume that the two communities in Northern Ireland have remained locked in a static relationship. The protestant community in particular has undergone a number of traumatic changes which has served to undermine the security of its position within the power structure of the province. The decline in traditional manufacturing industries in Northern Ireland, has been matched by a corresponding rise in unemployment among the skilled protestant working class. This is the class that has provided the bedrock of unionist support, which saw its economic self interest directly linked to the politics of union within the United Kingdom. The recent decline of unionist political influence may be traced from the suspension of the Northern Ireland parliament and the introduction of a system of direct rule from Westminster. The locally based government of Northern Ireland was a bastion of unionist supremacy from its inception in the 1920s. Thus it proved slow to react to the demands for catholic civil rights, slow to reform, and reluctant to move from the position where the state and its institutions were married in a commitment to unionist supremacy. Direct rule therefore sought to change the nature of institutional relationships with government which had united the protestant worker with the unionist governing class. It aimed to replace this set of traditional institutional relationships with a new set of objective, rational legal criteria. This decline of unionist influence has been further compounded by the 1987 Anglo Irish Agreement. This agreement, established between the Westminster government and the government of the Irish Republic, recognized formally for the first time the direct interest of the Irish government in the internal affairs of Northern Ireland. It provided a vehicle whereby the Irish government could play a part in influencing the composition, structure and development of the province's institutions. It offered a direct challenge to a unionist view of the province as completely separate from the Irish Republic.

The protestant community may therefore no longer occupy the powerful position that it held prior to the introduction of direct rule. These political changes have been married to institutional change. Brewer (1988) has noted a shift since 1969, from the "traditional" toward a more objective, rational model of policing within Northern Ireland. This "rationalist" model suggests that the nature of policing has shifted toward a more objective single standard of conduct against which all are policed. Brewer suggests that these changes have arisen as a result of British government influence under direct rule of the province. It is a recognition that the traditional association of the RUC with the state and unionist community resulted in isolation of the catholic minority from any sense of identification with the state and its police. Brewer argues that the RUC is able to maintain this

4

approach by constant reference to professional, objective policing standards, and the critical role of the British government as a neutral umpire.

There is therefore a dilemma at the heart of unionism. That is that the fight to defeat the violent forces of republicanism may ultimately require some compromise with the non violent political forces of republicanism. The very nature of compromise implies further erosion of the position and values of the protestant tradition. It is this dilemma and the institutional changes that have taken place within the province that have been the cause of much of the current alienation and anxiety that exists within the protestant community. The police remain however a product of the cultural values of the society from which it is formed and within which it operates. Northern Irish society is characterized by a diversity of irreducible views. The union has traditionally provided a vision of history and a view of the community's future. This adherence to a policing of unionist values has featured both as the basis of social order and has provided a meaning system which has confirmed the community and the RUC's position within it. A recognition of the nature of these social divisions in Northern Ireland remains an essential prerequisite for understanding the social and cultural identity of the police officer. This type of social structure imposes particular obligations and constraints upon policing. It places the police officer in a unique position in the social fabric of Northern Ireland where the officer may act to reinforce the values of the community to which he or she belongs. The essential question therefore is how far the attitudes of the police in Northern Ireland have changed from those supportive of the more traditional policing model of the era of local unionist government, toward support for a more contemporary model of policing? This study of the RUC reserve is therefore important since it examines whether the attitudes of an important segment of the RUC membership remain rooted within the traditional analysis of Northern Irish society.

This study of occupational culture starts from the recognition that work communities are not simply random aggregates of individual workers. It takes the position that the interpretation and meanings that individuals give to organizations depend on the social and cultural context within which these organizations have developed. Members of the part time RUC reserve live in the community and yet work throughout the year in counter terrorist operations in the province. They therefore require some conception of society and the forces that give it shape, in order for them to orientate their work. The ideas, both implicit and explicit that these police hold about society, help to formulate their views of what their job is all about. This is particularly critical in the context of a police force which has developed in a society dominated by major social division concerning the legitimacy of the state and the position occupied within it by the two main religious traditions.

Theory and method

Our understanding of Northern Irish society and the close interdependence of community institutions requires a research strategy which starts from the recognition of the cultural determination of meanings. People develop rules and norms of behaviour to assist them in their response to the external environment. These are passed from one generation to another and form part of the history and folk traditions of people working in the organization. They become recognized and internally acceptable patterns of conduct within the organization. These patterns of conduct represent explicit and implicit ways of affecting communication within the group, and develop a character or personality for an institution. The aim of this research is to uncover the meanings that social interaction holds for those participating in it. Explanations are then formulated from the stock of everyday knowledge from which these individual police officers derive their meanings.

The theoretical perspective employed in this research, therefore, uses the concept of social action, a concept which is fundamental to Weberian sociology. This suggests that the establishment of subjectively intended meaning forms the basis of a causal explanation of action (Weber 1974). Weber encourages us to ask questions about the validity of an existing social order and the basis on which that order rests and to what extent competing interpretations of legitimacy coexist. It is through the use of type constructs that the connections can be made between social action and its emphasis on the actor's definition of the structure of the organization.

The use of the action frame of reference represents a movement away from a dependence upon purely positivist strategies, toward a methodological strategy that fits the distinctiveness of social events. The positivist tradition of much research on organizational membership has as Dachler (1978) notes, produced conservative studies with an overriding concern with the status quo. This approach, Dachler argues has constrained us "from recognising questions about social phenomena and explicitly integrating into our explanations the many contradictions" (p. 51). Social action theory recognizes *inter alia*, that structures are for the most part created and sustained in interaction. This means that people develop a series of commonsense constructs to enable them to preselect and preinterpret the world which they experience as the reality of their daily lives. The constructs used by the social scientist in order to grasp this

6

reality have to be grounded upon the thought objects constructed by the commonsense thinking of people.

This book therefore follows a developing tradition of social action research within the police (see for example Cain 1973, Reiner 1978, and Brewer 1991). The social action perspective is, as Thompson (1967) notes only a loose label for a broad range of approaches, a continuum from ethnomethodology to systems theory, what Goldthorpe (1973) recognizes as the modern equivalent of the *Natur* and *Geisteswissenschaften* theme in German sociology. The debate between the positivist approach of systems theory and pure *verstehen* is not, however one of absolutes but rather a question of the degree of dependence which the researcher attaches to positivist techniques. A recognition of the ethnomethodologic position that our central concern is social action should not deny the existence of other phenomena which exist independent of social action and yet have a bearing on our understanding of meaning (demographic factors, for example). A particular concern of this research therefore is to provide a balance between observation and discussion and statistical methods of enquiry.

One of the major concerns therefore of this research is to develop "type constructs" of behaviour by a study of the meanings which actors attach to their behaviour. It is through the use of type constructs that the connections can be made between social action and differing meaning systems. Through these type constructs it is possible to pose questions about the nature of the organization and its future. This places the study of the part time RUC reserve within the mainstream of police studies; many studies of the police have produced typologies of police behaviour that have developed around a particular police culture (see for example the work of: Broderick 1974, Reiner 1978, Muir 1977).

The research suggests however that this study of the part time RUC reserve does not fit easily into the context of studies of the police in the rest of the United Kingdom. Throughout Britain there is not the pattern of occupational segregation and social structure that is evident in Northern Ireland. The study of policing in Northern Ireland may have a more superficial similarity to other societies subject to similar ethnic and social division. Thus Reiser (1983) suggests that the police in Israel are subject to similar pressures and influences, (see also Gurvitch 1971, Besinger 1981), whilst a similar mix of social and religious issues lies at the root of some European societies such as the Netherlands (see Goudsblom 1967, Knijt 1959, Windmuller 1969, and Albeda 1977), or Belgium (Lorwin 1970). Within Europe, many societies may well possess strong ethnic division. However these societies are held together by a common identification with the notion of the state itself. In

Northern Ireland it is the very legitimacy of the state which is subject to direct challenge.

Brewer (1991) outlines many of the research problems associated with police research in general and research within the RUC in particular. Two distinct research problems, acceptance of the researcher by the organization in order to gain entry, and the need for the researcher to maintain detachment and objectivity to ensure validity of the research, are accentuated by the nature of policing in Northern Ireland and the consequent requirement for a high degree of security. For this research, the process of entry into the organization was slow and tortuous, and took two years from initial discussions with force personnel to the eventual granting of permission for the research. It required the identification of key gate keepers in the organization, and convincing them of the merit of the research. I never met the chief constable, but permission for me to carry out research was gained from the chief constable on my behalf by senior force officers. An inspector who was serving as a staff officer at police headquarters was then given the responsibility of liaising with me.

The survey

It was clear from the outset that any purely statistical analysis of attitudes within the part time force would not be sufficient alone to explain the social dynamics inherent in membership of the force. It would have been unable to elucidate the crucial aspects - the reasons why people join the force on a part time basis and the meanings which they attach to their membership and behaviour in the organization. It was therefore recognized from the start of the research that some form of interview and discussion process should take place with the officers themselves. An ideal situation would have been a period of full participant observation with the part time force. This was not thought practical or necessary in this instance as I had already spent a number of years prior to this research working alongside members of the force. Also the context of security work in the province would have limited participant observation to often non contentious activities within the safety of police bases.

A postal survey of social attitudes alone would however have been politically less contentious than other methods and may have allowed the force greater control over the questioning nature, and direction of the research. A postal questionnaire was developed (see appendix). It contained a range of questions covering both demographic information and information on political and social attitudes. It is a matter of great credit to the force, and courage on the part of my liaison officer, that no attempt was made to suggest modification or moderation of the survey coverage. The questionnaire was piloted with a small sample of officers, and as a result two further questions concerning the Police Federation were incorporated.

A questionnaire was sent to all part time RUC who were on the establishment at July 1990. Replies were returned from 891 part time police. This represents a 57 per cent response rate. This varied between 75 per cent in N division to 34 per cent in L division. The part time police are not an homogeneous work force. It was recognized from the outset of this research that geographic location would provide a key variable in understanding attitudes. Responses from police divisions were therefore amalgamated into three shorthand categories: divisions A, D and E are referred to throughout the text in the shorthand category of "Belfast". divisions H, L and N are referred to as "border", and division G, J, K, P and O as "country". (It should also be noted that soon after commencing this research the boundaries of some police divisions were slightly modified.)

Table 1.1
Response by division

Police division	Total P/T	Number of respondents	% response
G	159	75	47
H	85	52	61
J	121	82	68
K	46	32	70
L	145	50	34
N	32	24	75
O	83	57	69
P	137	50	37
A	225	123	55
D	285	188	66
E	254	158	62
Total	1,572	891	57

9

It can be assumed that the respondents are a random selection from the population. At the 95 per cent level of confidence, population parameters may be estimated to within ±2.21 per cent.

The main impression is that in certain divisions, the part time reserve are an aging population. Thirty four per cent of respondents were aged over 45 years. Similarly 21 per cent were aged over 50 years. Recruitment literature suggests that whereas 62 is the retirement age for the part time RUC, it is unusual for people to see service beyond 57 years. Table 1.2 shows that in the Border divisions, there is little evidence that the high age profile of part time police is being reduced by new young recruits.

Table 1.2
Age distribution of part time RUC

Age	Belfast %	Border %	Country %
Up to 30 years	26	13	24
30-39 years	28	28	28
40-49 years	27	31	28
Over 50 years	19	28	20
Total number	469	126	296

In the border stations, only 13 per cent of the part time RUC are aged under 30, whereas 38 per cent of the border sample are aged over 50 years. This may reflect a reluctance of the RUC to recruit part time members in border areas because of the attendant security problems that arise for part time police living in the border areas. It may also suggest that fewer people actively seek to join the part time force, in these areas.

The image of a relatively aging part time RUC workforce is essentially a male phenomenon. Females represent 37 per cent of the overall part time RUC workforce and are much more heavily represented in the younger age groupings. Thirty one per cent of females are aged under 30 years, compared to 21 per cent of male part time police. Table 1.3 shows that border stations have a smaller percentage of women part time police than other divisions.

Table 1.3
Sex distribution of part time RUC

	Belfast	Border	Country
Number of females	118	27	94
Number of respondents	469	126	296
% Female	25%	21%	32%

It is in the country divisions where there are few recruitment problems, and where there is the highest percentage of women part time police.

Further confirmation of the age difference between the sexes is reflected in the data on marital status: only 17 per cent of male respondents are single. This contrasts with 42 per cent of female respondents. Female respondents may however have more unstable domestic circumstances: 3 per cent of male part time police are separated or divorced. This compares to 8 per cent of female part time police. This is a mean divorce and separation rate which is higher for women than the Northern Ireland figure of 4.39 per cent of the population who are divorced or separated. The sample is broadly reflective of Northern Irish household size. The average Northern Irish family size for households with children under 16 in 1989/90 is 4.35. Fifty two per cent of part time RUC are in households of between 3 and 4 occupants.

Workers both part time and full time in all organizations evolve an operational code for managing the interface between organizational constraint and individual attitudes and behaviour. This operational code, the set of meanings with which individuals face the world, are in part a function of the work position, class and religious position in which the individual exists. The police, therefore, to be representative of the society which they police, may aim to draw their recruits from as broad a representative band of work, class and religious categories as possible. It is clear that in some notable respects the part time RUC are not reflective of Northern Irish society as a whole. They are for example more heavily concentrated than the broad spread of the population in social classes I and II.

A considerable amount of time was devoted to the problem of non response. The non response was compounded by the nature of this part time work. The work is such that people may be able to move into and out of employment more readily than if the work formed the primary income source. Therefore at any one point in time the survey was likely to encounter a number of non active part time police officers who may be in the process of leaving the force. It is estimated by the RUC that this may account for about 8 per cent of the total manpower figure for part time officers. Moreover the nature of the work suggests that some officers may devote a minimal number of hours per month to policing, and may therefore have missed the return date for the questionnaire. In these instances considerable effort was devoted to contacting these people and seeking their support. In addition to personal exhortations to particular stations, reminder letters were sent to all non respondents.

Police officers possess a natural suspicion of those from outside the organization who ask questions concerning their employment. This may be true of police officers generally, but holds particular relevance in the context of Northern Ireland. Concern about the security implications of this enquiry held centre stage in all the deliberations of those involved in the survey. This matter was managed in part through the normal processes of survey management. It soon became clear that research management would require more than the single liaison officer working with me, but would require the support of those officers at RUC headquarters who were responsible for the management of the reserve force. Their able assistance and support enabled them to handle directly many of the enquiries from officers concerning confidentiality, and to deal directly with the problem of non response. The involvement of the reserve office ensured that the nature of the research was given wide publicity among the part time reservists prior to the distribution of the questionnaire. The research was outlined in the force's own bulletin, and was discussed at the consultative liaison committee meetings held on a regular basis between the management of the RUC and representatives of the part time reservists. I also ensured that the Police Federation was aware of my research aims and were in broad support of my activities. It was also decided that distribution and retrieval of questionnaires should be through the police department with responsibility for the part time force. It was my view that this decision would go some way toward allaying the fears of those officers who were concerned about information going direct to the University of Ulster or, more significantly the names and locations of part time police officers being accessible to members of the University. Thus the questionnaire was printed at the university, a covering letter issued on university paper, the coding and subsequent analysis was carried out at the university. However the questionnaires were distributed through the force's mail system, and returned to the reserve office to be forwarded to me. Once the data on the questionnaire had been transcribed to the computer the questionnaires were returned to the reserve office for shredding. Thus although the non response may appear somewhat high, I believe that all the possible steps were taken to minimize the problem.

The interviews

Reservists' attitudes and behaviour toward the society in which they live and the policing which they undertake are inextricably intertwined with where they live and the degree of isolation or residential segregation that exists between themselves and their catholic neighbour. This occupational culture is defined and reinforced by the process of narrative and verbal communication. Holdaway (1983) notes that studies of police culture underline the importance of this folk narrative as a means of defining and reinforcing this culture. It was therefore important to conduct interviews with officers from contrasting areas. Three areas were identified. Interviews were first conducted with reservists who live and work along the border region. This is a region that is characterized by a succession of small isolated protestant and catholic communities. It is an area that has been renowned for its violent sectarian activity where communities often feel a high degree of isolation and surrounding hostility. The region stands in contrast to Belfast. Belfast is best described as a series of separate cohesive identifiable communities often defined by location and religion. They are often communities facing the problems of urban decay and growing unemployment. The third area from which interviews were conducted lacks the urban characteristics of Belfast or the isolated community identities of the border area. Interviews were conducted in Newtownabbey and Bangor. These are the dormitory areas to Belfast located respectively in the traditionally protestant areas of North Down and South Antrim. Unlike their two counter parts these dormitory areas do not face the problems of urban violence and decay, or the problems of community decline. These are areas that may lack the strong ties that bind the communities of the city and border.

Different problems of non response are raised by the interview process. It is impossible to know who made a positive decision to refuse to take part in the interview process and who was simply unavailable on the night selected. The interview process required me to identify a number of police stations and to arrange through the reserve office a suitable date to spend the evening at the station with the part time officers. I was not therefore privy to any discussion or debate at station level concerning my imminent arrival and motives for my research. I therefore devoted a considerable

13

amount of time at each location explaining who I was and the nature of my research.

A total of 56 officers were interviewed in 10 police stations. The officers that formed part of this taped programme were not chosen at random but were those on duty and available at the time of my arrival. The choice of police station determined who was likely to be approached. No claim is made therefore that this interview programme is statistically representative of the part time force as a whole. Stations were selected by me on the basis that the nature of policing varied according to location. They were therefore chosen to represent a cross section of police activity within the province. Thus four stations were selected that were situated along the Border, four stations were selected from North and West Belfast, and two large stations were selected from the relatively peaceful commuter areas of Co Down and Antrim. In addition to selecting the stations I was concerned that my interviews should include female officers; a total of 17 female officers were interviewed. All the interviews were taped and lasted an average of three hours at each station.

I considered it important not to depend solely on a predetermined question agenda, but rather to record discussion as it developed over a range of issues, some of which had been identified by the earlier questionnaire, some of which had been thrown up by the events of the preceding week. At each location I made free use of the tape recorder; discussions and activities were taped and later transcribed into a word processing format. I always introduced the tape recorder simply as a research tool and always offered the facility for it to be turned off. Occasionally officers did ask for their views not to be recorded but this was in a very small minority of cases. The process of taping was central to the research process. It enabled me to form part of the discussion process rather than remaining isolated behind a pen and pad. It also enabled me to obtain some understanding of the meanings police officers often attached to their views and opinions. Such meanings often form an essential ingredient of the discussion that may take place around an issue. A rich vein of ethnographic material emerged from these tapes. It would be impossible to include all that was said, rather, the book attempts to bring together a number of commonly identified themes and issues.

Conclusion

One of the key notions that has informed this study of part time reservists is the manner in which the reservists' sense of who they are, their social identity derives from a range of influences. RUC reservists derive this sense of identity from their understanding of the nature of community, their full time work, family and leisure activities. The book therefore sets out to explore these influences.

There is a history of part time commitment to security in Northern Ireland that is unique in the British Isles. It sets the part time officer apart from full time colleagues. It also ensures that those becoming part time officers become part of an occupational culture rooted in the traditions of part time defence of the Northern Ireland state. Chapter 2 therefore explores this history and the relevance that it holds for contemporary policing. The chapter describes the origins of the part time RUC reserve, the disbandment of the USC (B Specials), and the reasons for membership of the reserve. The chapter draws upon the experiences of older members of the force many of whom had experience as B Specials, and looks at their attitudes toward the disbandment of this force. The chapter looks at the empirical data on the reasons for joining the RUC reserve, and recounts many officers early experiences of joining and the impact on their families and friendship patterns.

Chapter three concentrates on the interview data to describe the attitudes toward the tasks associated with policing. The chapter explores the importance of station and workgroup in the formation of attitudes toward work. The chapter also looks at the specific problems faced by women in the reserve. It examines the attitudes of women toward the arming of females, the motivations of women police and the problems that they may encounter in a predominantly masculine environment.

The establishment and maintenance of a part time support element to the RUC provides a direct means of community support for the police. In a society where policing is dominated by the threat of inter community violence and insurgency, the existence of a part time support force enables individuals in society to translate into socially acceptable behaviour, views that may be held about the nature of community conflict and the role of the state. Chapter four describes the social and occupational background of part time police officers. The chapter looks at their friendship patterns, and families and describes the impact of their work on their family life. It looks at the attitudes of employers toward the RUC reserve and explores some of the dangers experienced by officers in the interface between policing and the community in which they live.

The existence of a significant part time contingent of police may act as a direct assistance to police and community relations. The part time police by virtue of their full time employment within the community, may be seen as acting as a bridge between the full time police organization and the wider community. This final justification may only be true at a very general level of abstraction. This study shows that part time police particularly in Belfast, may often not police the immediate community in which they live. The study also shows that for security reasons, many may not be known in their own community as part time police. However at a more general level their continuing experience of full time employment outside of the RUC and life in the community may provide for the full time police a sounding board of public opinion. The final part of the book is therefore devoted to an exploration of the social identity and attitudes of part time police officers. Both quantitative and interview data are drawn on to provide an insight into the range of social and political attitudes that are held by reservists. The distinctions that exist between the attitudes of the reserve and the wider community are examined and the chapter explores the attitudes of the force toward the issues of community relations, and the specific problems that are faced by catholic members. The wider political attitudes of the RUC reserve in the context of political issues in Northern Ireland, the views of the RUC reserve toward relations with the Irish Republic, the issues of law and order and the general field of security policy are examined. A typology of policing in Northern Ireland is then developed. The occupational culture of the RUC reserve imposes a number of recruitment and training imperatives upon the organization. These are explored in the context of the future role of the RUC reserve.

References

Albeda, W. (1977), Changing industrial relations in the Netherlands, *Industrial relations*, Vol. 16, pp. 1-14.

Bent, A. (1974), *The Politics of law reform Lexington*.

Bessinger, G. (1981), Israeli police in transition, *Police studies*, Summer pp. 3-8.

Brewer, J. (1988), *Police public order and the state*, Macmillan.

Brewer, J. and Magee, K. (1991), *Inside the RUC*, OUP.

Cain, M. (1973), *Society and the policeman's role*, Rouledge, Kegan, and Paul.

16

Dachler, M. and Wilpert, B. (1978), Conceptual dimensions and boundaries of participation in organizations, *Administrative science quarterly*, Vol. 23, pp. 1-39.

Elliot, R. and Hickie, J. (1971), *Ulster a case study in conflict*, Longman.

Goldthorpe, J. (1973), A revolution in sociology? *Sociology*, Vol. 7, pp. 449-462.

Goudsblom, J. (1967), *Dutch society*, New York.

Gurvitch, M. (1971), The Image of the police in Israel, *Law and society review*, Vol. 5, pp. 367-387.

Holdaway, S. (1983), *Inside the British police - a force at work*, Blackwell.

Knijt, J. (1959), *Influences of denominationalism*, Archives de sociologie des religions iv, No. 8, pp. 105-111.

Lorwin, V. (1971), Segmented pluralism, ideological cleavages and political cohesion in smaller European democracies, *Comparative politics*, Vol. 3, pp. 141-175.

Manning, P. and Butler, A. (1982), Perceptions of police authority, *Police journal*, Vol. 55, No. 82 pp. 333-344.

Reiner, R. (1978), *The blue coated worker*, Cambridge University press.

Reiner, R. (1982), Who are the police? *Political quarterly*, Vol. 53:2, pp. 165-180.

Reiner, R. (1985), *The politics of the police*, Wheatsheaf.

Reiser, G. Israeli police politics and profiles, *Police studies*, Vol. 6, No 1 pp. 27-35.

Thompson, J. (1967), *Organizations in action*, New York, McGraw Hill.

Tonnies, F. (1971), *Community and society*, OUP.

Windmuller, B. (1969), *Labour relations in the Netherlands*, Attica.

Weber, M. (1974), *The theory of social and economic organization,* Oxford University Press.

2 The origins of the part time RUC reserve

Introduction

There is a long tradition in Northern Ireland of paid, local part time policing. This tradition starts from the very emergence of the state itself, when from its inception its very existence was threatened by communal violence. This chapter describes the development of the Northern Ireland state, and traces the emergence of the RUC reserve as the inheritors of this tradition. This chapter shows how the attitudes and beliefs that were associated with part time policing in the 1920s still form part of the history and folk traditions of the modern organisation. The part time reserve still contains a number of officers now rapidly declining, whose experience traces back to the last days of the reserves' predecessor organisation. The chapter therefore looks at their views and shows how the core beliefs of these officers compare with many of the views of contemporary recruits to the reserves.

The social structure of Northern Ireland outlined in Chapter one, has grown in tandem with the political and economic structuring of the Northern Irish state. By 1919 the political situation in Ireland was such as to be of serious concern to the northern unionist tradition. Unionism in the North of Ireland, unlike the south had become a powerful economic and social force. The Orange Order with its strong working class following, had by the 1920s become fully integrated into the political processes of unionism. Tierney (1978) argues that by 1919 unionism as a political force had shifted its ground. The defence of the union of Great Britain with the whole of Ireland had become directly related to the defence of protestantism and ultimately the defence of a union of Great Britain with the predominantly protestant north of Ireland. The pre 1914 proposals by the

British government for home rule were by force of events now redundant. In 1920 the government moved toward proposals which culminated in the 1920 Government of Ireland Act. This Act provided for the establishment of two governments in Ireland with the (somewhat pious) hope of ultimate unification.

Ulster unionists embarked therefore reluctantly upon a course of internal self government. Oliver (1978) notes that the setting up of a Northern government was "no joyous occasion, no happy culmination of national aspirations".

No politician had been campaigning for a separate state. To the unionists the settlement represented a second best, a barely acceptable substitute for continued full integration with Britain. The establishment of a Northern Ireland state had two immediate and profound effects. Firstly, northern nationalists refused to accept partition and secondly, the unionist majority continued to see itself as a beleaguered grouping isolated within a northern enclave of a catholic island. The Act had effectively translated into geographic and political reality, the ethnic and cultural divisions of the island and created what was referred to in 1934 by Lord Craigavon as "a protestant parliament for a protestant people".

Politics, culture and the ensuing social structure thus became set in an ethnically divided pattern. The existence of these divisions served to reinforce the relationship between unionism and protestantism, nationalism and catholicism. It has produced a unique social structure, and at times, high levels of politically inspired violence.

The emergent civil unrest in the south of Ireland after 1918 led the Westminster government to create a number of auxiliary forces to support the beleaguered Royal Irish Constabulary and the British army. The government response in the north of the country was to establish in 1920 an Ulster Service Corps (USC). Farrell (1983) notes that this decision rationalized a number of adhoc measures that had been taken by local councils which had set up local volunteer forces in places such as Lisburn and Belfast. The establishment of the USC was the natural result of unionists feeling threatened by a developing threat of the Irish Republican Army (IRA) and a mistrust of British government intentions toward unionists in the North of Ireland.

The B Specials

The USC was to be under the ultimate command of the police divisional commissioner, however the USC had its own command structure, and in the case of the B Specials had their own district and sub district commandants. The USC was to consist of three sections:

A Specials, a full time force engaged on six monthly contracts, paid at the same rate as the RIC dressed and equipped exactly as the RIC.

B Specials were to be a part time force undertaking guard and patrol duties. They were to be unpaid although in receipt of a yearly allowance. They could be called out for full time duty in an emergency. They operated solely within their own locality, were armed, and were able to keep their arms at home.

C Specials were to be a reserve force with no regular duties and were intended to be used merely in emergency when they could be called out either on a part time or full time basis.

The Royal Ulster Constabulary was established by the Constabulary Act (NI) of 1922. It was a modified version of the RIC. Brewer (1988) notes that it was established with the aim of developing a significant catholic presence within the force. The contested nature of the state, and the fragile peace of that period resulted in little catholic recruitment to a force which maintained and developed its paramilitary role.

Throughout the period of transition from the Royal Irish Constabulary to the establishment of the Royal Ulster Constabulary in 1922, the USC bore a major burden of responsibility for the enforcement of law and order in the province. It was only by the early 1930s that conditions had moderated sufficiently to allow most of the A and all of the C Specials to be stood down leaving only the B Specials still in existence.

At no point in Northern Ireland's turbulent history was it considered strategically possible, or politically desirable to disband this locally recruited part time force. Part time B Specials continued to patrol throughout the post war period and provided a major resource to the RUC during the IRA campaign of the 1950s. This was local community volunteer support for a state threatened by the same forces that had threatened it from its inception. The tasks of the B Specials were mainly the protection of key installations against sabotage and patrolling of the border and their local areas.

There remains an inherent contradiction in the attitudes that many of the older reservists hold about the B Specials. On the one hand there remains a constant and continual theme of success; the B Specials were seen as the successful arm of the security forces. This was the organisation that had held the line in the 1920s and was responsible for keeping republican military activity curbed in subsequent years. There is also a recognition however that such success was at a price. It was these tasks of patrolling local areas that inevitably bought the B Specials into direct conflict with the local catholic population. In communities where name may denote religion, and religion may denote political allegiance, being stopped and questioned by a patrol of local B Specials may well have been seen as harassment and generated catholic hostility and alienation from the state:

> ... There certainly seemed to be a large fear element about the B Specials which isn't with us (The RUCR) I don't think. Society has changed ... If we (The USC) were not liked its because we were good at our job. I always remember people saying years ago, you couldn't have gone from one town to another without being stopped by the B Specials especially the country routes. (Country reservist)

> ... Oh, I was 25 years on the B Specials, so I'm old now. They just operated much the same as the police, only there was a platoon here or there every three or four miles throughout the country and they knew everything there was, they had the local knowledge. The B Specials they were in the country all the time and if anything happened they knew all about it and would know he was a stranger. (Border reservist)

> ... Well I joined the security forces at a very early age in fact I joined in 1950, it was the old USC. I was working in Enniskillen at the time and it was quite near the border and there was always an influx of undesirables as they were called and a lot of the people joined for their own protection and trying to protect others as well of course, and that's really what it amounted to. ... They (the B Specials) were very effective to the point that they had a great local knowledge - if any stranger was seen in the area everyone wanted to know who he was, what he was about and where he came from, and that's where the B Specials scored because they knew everybody in their own area - local knowledge was a great thing. (Border reservist)

There remained at the root of this part time service a strong sense of community identity and status. The USC provided one of the institutions which underscored political allegiance. It provided a male bonding structure which reinforced the values of state and Crown allegiance against a seemingly hostile and republican world. It performed in one organisation many of the social functions associated with church, orange order and political membership. The nature and function of values and ideologies in the state acted as a buttress to, and served as justifications for, organisational behaviour.

... I probably like many others felt it was a bitter blow, a let down to Northern Ireland to the fact the B Specials was phased out. Having said that I have no regrets being in the USC, I was very proud because I was involved in a country platoon, where people were farmers, and there was a tremendous social aspect as well, and community involvement we all knew each other and got on well, and we thought we were doing something to protect the community. (Border reservist)

... I'm one of the older ones here. I first joined the Specials in 1949 a fortnight before I was 18. At that stage I joined simply because my friends joined. I was in the Belfast Platoon ... I thought I was doing something useful for the community, and it was expected of me then ... Nor can I turn round and point a finger and say that what we did was 100 per cent wrong. (Belfast reservist)

... you've got to understand, where I came from it was the natural thing to do. Our family were always in it. (Country reservist)

Throughout the post war period the USC provided the main manpower support to the RUC. The regular patrolling in the face of a real or perceived threat from the IRA acted as a constant reminder to members of the catholic population of the religious and political division within Northern Ireland. It also demonstrated that this was a division reinforced by an armed and apparently independent protestant force.

The 1922 Special Powers Act which survived until 1972, gave the RUC powers against those it considered were subverting the state. It was therefore a legislative instrument that focused exclusively upon the catholic community. It also ensured that the RUC was considered by the catholic community to be an instrument of unionist rule assisting in the upholding of a protestant ascendency. This Act formed an important aspect of the civil rights campaigning of the late 1960s.

The political and social isolation felt by the catholic community led inexorably to the civil rights demonstrations of the late 1960s and to the subsequent bitter sectarian rioting. Hezlet (1972) notes that by August 1969 the civil disturbances had become such that both the RUC and the USC were exhausted from constant pressure arising from sectarian riots. The RUC was completely unprepared for this level of sectarian rioting. It was ill equipped and inadequately trained to manage the sudden violent and continuous rioting of this period. It is therefore unsurprising that faced with this mounting pressure it drew more and more on the support of its reserve forces. This support developed until the B Specials found themselves confronting urban rioting far removed from the patrolling activity with which they were so familiar, rioting for which it was clearly untrained:

> ... I remember the first time of the troubles I was in the Specials and we were rushed to the Boyne bridge, now that was to make sure that the Sandy Row crowd didn't come over it and it was a fixed point for months, I remember the shots being fired from the top of Divis flats that night and we were on the corner of the Grosvenor Road and Sandy Row. Now that was to stop the protestants attacking the catholics, the way you hear it nowadays you would think we were there organising them! (the protestants). (Belfast reservist)

> ... we were there the whole night, the B Specials knew who they were looking for, because mainly all B Specials were stationed in their local areas. We knew who we were looking for, that was the problem we were too good that's why they (the catholic community) didn't like us around. (Border reservist)

> ... At the height of the troubles here I did a lot of duty down round here and if you went into a crowd and were able to name 4 or 5 of them fellahs you never had any problem, but if you went into even a crowd of six and you didn't know one of them you could have been in trouble. (Belfast reservist)

The RUC were one of the principle casualties of the civil campaigning of the late 1960s. The months of July and August 1969 placed the police and the B Specials under extreme pressure and public scrutiny. On the 14 August 1969, the Northern Ireland government requested that the British government introduce troops to maintain law and order on the streets. The use of the B Specials to assist the police in this situation had been at a cost. The B Specials, pushed to the front line became exposed to public scrutiny and criticism. On 20 August 1969, the army took over security responsibility and the USC was transferred to military command. There was clear anxiety on the part of the B Specials that the introduction of military command would remove the B Specials traditional freedom of activity within its communities and lead to its curtailment and ultimate disbandment.

Later that same month, the military commander in Northern Ireland issued a message to all members of the USC stating that there was no intention to disband the Corps, or disarm it. The USC had however been the subject of considerable criticism particularly from the catholic community concerning its role in the civil unrest. The first serious criticism of the USC came from the Cameron Report (1969) which alleged that B Specials were present in protestant crowds at riots. The report also states: "We have good ground for inferring that in the ranks of the Ulster protestant volunteer force are numbered members of the USC".

This criticism of the part played in riots by the USC, and the failure of the RUC to contain the civil unrest led the government in Westminster to look closely at policing in the province. Reform of the RUC became one of the objectives of British government policy. It followed criticism of the RUC in the 1969 Cameron Commission and the Scarman Tribunal of the same year. The government established an advisory committee chaired by Lord Hunt to examine:

> ... recruitment organisation structure and composition of the Royal Ulster Constabulary and the Ulster Special constabulary and their respective functions and to recommend what changes are required to provide for the efficient enforcement of law and order in Northern Ireland.

The Hunt report of 1969 highlighted what it regarded as the anachronistic nature of policing in Northern Ireland. It sought to reform the RUC by removing its paramilitary responsibilities, and establishing a force based upon an archetypical model of policing in Great Britain. The Report added fuel to the criticisms of the USC by noting:

> ... whilst there is no law or official rule that precludes any person, whatever his religion from joining the USC, the fact remains that for a variety of reasons no roman catholic is a member.

The report argued that the duties undertaken by the USC are mainly military in character. The committee saw considerable merit in the continuing presence of a local force with local knowledge. The report proposed that a new locally recruited force should be established under military command, to be called the Ulster Defence Regiment (UDR). This force together with a new police volunteer reserve should replace the USC.

The new RUC part time reserve

The proposal for a volunteer police reserve had much in common with the role of the special constabularies that exist in the rest of the

United Kingdom. It bore little resemblance to the USC and represented a clear attempt by government to move away from the tradition of volunteer protestant armed support for the RUC. The report argued that the proposed reserve should be unpaid, unarmed, and wear only a similar uniform to their full time colleagues. The report noted the suggestion that the new police reserve should have a title different from that of special constabulary, because of the hostility that such a title has in certain areas. The report argued that whatever its name: "special efforts should be made to achieve the participation of members of minority groups". (para 108)

In the place of the old B Specials were formed two organisations. A part time police reserve and a mainly part time military force. This latter force was established as the Ulster Defence Regiment (UDR). The purpose of the UDR was to undertake the military tasks associated with patrolling the border and guarding key installations. The UDR was to be under military command with officers from the rest of the British army. Part time assistance to the police took the title of the RUC reserve.

The part time RUC reserve was established in 1970. The RUC reserve were to be subject to two weeks full time initial police training. This training was to be followed by regular monthly training and run in conjunction with training in the use of firearms. The attempt to develop an unarmed RUC failed in the face of a growing terrorist campaign. The RUC reserve therefore, like its full time colleagues became an armed force almost from its inception. The structure of the part time police ensured that after initial training the part time RUC reservists would not become involved in attending sensitive domestic disputes, issues of a confidential nature or riot duties. Unlike the former B Specials, there was to be no separate command structure. The RUC reservist would therefore remain at the rank of constable. The work of the reservists was to be allocated to part time police on the basis of a duty roster compiled by a full time station sergeant with specific responsibility for the part time police.

The RUC required the potential reservist to be in good health, with good eyesight, and able to pass a standard entrance test of intellect. Once the reservist passed through recruit training the officer was to be subject to two years' probation. It was established from the outset that during service the officer should refrain from political activity, and could resign with one month's notice. An early decision was taken to pay reservists for their police work. This was to compensate them for any loss of earnings and to recognize the significant number of work hours required of the reserve. The current pay for the reservist is almost £5 per hour with an annual special duty allowance of £300.

Recruitment for both the UDR and the part time RUC reserve started almost immediately. It was hoped that the new organisations would recruit both from the catholic population and from those former members of the USC who wished to continue their service. The proposals amounted however, to the effective disbandment of the USC. Many members of the USC considered that they were becoming the scapegoats for the wider political failings of the unionist government. This resulted in many feeling isolated and betrayed, and caused considerable resentment amongst its ranks:

... The B Specials actually had no equipment only an old rifle, and the old 303 and I reckon if they had have kept the B Specials on and spent the same amount of money on the B Specials as they did on the UDR they would have had a good force because a lot of good men were in at that time - we have been betrayed now, that's it, no more! (switches off tape recorder). (Border reservist)

... There was a strong sense of betrayal, yes. We held the ring against people working to destroy the state ... I would have to say yes a sense of betrayal and having been let down. (Border reservist)

... The disbanding of the Specials was a very sore point and we had several meetings on it, John Taylor met us. He was the only MP that would meet us and discuss it. We had meetings in Ballymena, Hillsborough, Portadown and Bangor but we all decided here we weren't going to join anything else and then one by one we just relented and joined the part time reserve. But we were let down, badly let down. (Country reservist)

... I had been in the B Specials for two years but I had not intended to join the security forces again, not after the way they treated the specials, but the sheer volume of violence there was at the time, I felt I had to join again, and that was my only reason for joining. (Belfast reservist)

... The last 18 months of the Specials was very heavy here, they agreed to pay us 9 shillings an hour and you could do as many nights as you wanted, we had 18 men to supply each night for guard duty, over the gas works, government buildings and covered the water line at Newforge and 18 men each night was some covering to get them covered a month in advance, but the men worked very well. I think everyone had felt the strain of the troubles, but it was the Specials holding everything together. Then I went onto the reserve, the same station sergeant was here and I did the same job, just a different uniform but you couldn't escape it, this feeling we'd been let down, done our job too well and had to be brought into line. (Belfast reservist)

The RUC reserve was therefore to be a new beginning, a new organisation with a more direct policing role, yet maintaining the opportunity for wide community involvement in the maintenance of law and order. The new organisation may attract new recruits, it was however largely peopled from the ranks of the old B Specials. The informal rules and norms of behaviour in the new RUC reserve inevitably held some linkage to significant past events, and the members of the RUC reserve thereby become imbued with the organisations' history. These attitudes are passed from one generation to another and form part of the history and folk traditions of people working in the organisation. They assist in the development of a character or personality for the institution and in the officers response to the external environment. It has a direct affect upon its recruitment.

Workers both part time and full time in all organizations evolve an operational code for managing the interface between organizational constraint and individual attitudes and behaviour. This operational code, the set of meanings with which indiviudals face the world, are in part a function of the work position, class and religious position in which the individual exists. The police, therefore, to be representative of the society which they police, may aim to draw their recruits from as broad a representative band of work, class and religious categories as possible. It is clear that in some notable respects the part time RUC are not reflective of Northern Irish society as a whole. They are for example more heavily concentrated than the broad spread of the population in social classes I and II.

The recruitment process is therefore central to the harmonisation of values and the perpetuation of certain sets of key attitudes. The recruitment process ensures that the right "type" of person is recruited, one who subscribes to these values. It may therefore be that the RUC reserve is a prisoner of its own folk history. The research shows that despite the aspirations identified at its inception, the RUC reserve has conspicuously failed to achieve a religious balance to its recruitment. Ninety five per cent of all survey respondents. answered the question concerning religious affiliation. Table 2.1 shows that the part time RUC reserve is a markedly protestant force:

28

Table 2.1
Religious composition of the part time RUC
compared with the Northern Ireland population

Denomination	Part time RUC %	Northern Ireland* %
Roman catholic	3	36
Presbyterian	39	23
Anglican	26	18
Other protestant	16	8
Christian non specific	9	2
None	6	12

* *Source: NISAS*

The importance of religion in Northern Irish life is underscored by the fact that church attendance is far higher in Northern Ireland than almost anywhere else in the United Kingdom or Europe. Church attendance provides an important indication of the strength of religious identity and the inter active influence of respondent and neighbour in reinforcing attitudinal positions. Table 2.2 shows that the part time police have a weekly church attendance pattern similar to the Northern Ireland population as a whole:

Table 2.2
Church attendance of part time RUC

% Attending church

Location	Weekly	Monthly	Annually	Rarely/never
Belfast	45	16	17	22
Border	63	22	9	6
Country	55	19	13	13

Religious identity expressed in terms of attendance is far higher among part time reservists working in border stations, where over 60 per cent

29

attend church on a weekly or fortnightly basis, compared with 45 per cent in the Belfast area.

The part time RUC reserve is therefore a strongly protestant group. It has moved little from the protestant domination of its former B Specials. This may result in a sub culture of hostility toward catholic recruitment, a set of values and norms that associate catholicism with republicanism and opposition to the forces of unionism. There is a clear lack of trust among many existing members of the part time RUC reserve toward any members of the catholic community that may wish to join:

> ... Also, certain things condemn them, you see, some will collect the dole money but they won't put on the cap and the crown and wear it, they don't have the same attitude to the state of Northern Ireland itself, well, I mean, if they are not for the state of Northern Ireland as separate from Southern Ireland perhaps they don't want to be associated with the crown forces ... (Border reservist)

> ... In this station in the old days there never was a catholic policeman because they have to deal with people in Sandy Row and they are kind of hostile to that, Probably as well they wouldn't be a hundred per cent trusted by his own comrades because a man from the IRA could join the security forces. (Belfast reservist)

> ... Well, catholics are always from early day nationalist orientated and still are and they're not interested in taking any part in Ulster and that's still very much the case. Only a small minority would join but its too dangerous even for them to do it. The catholics basically represent nationalists, they want a united Ireland and they are not too keen on Britain. Then their church and what they are taught is to do with it too. (Country reservist)

> ... Then of course, you might be suspicious of them as well, that's another problem, they may not be trusted it doesn't matter how well you know them, there maybe a few informers, I mean, I would encourage them by all means to join, but you would never get the men to join. (Belfast reservist)

Attitudes toward the recruitment of individual catholics become further reinforced by general perceptions of the catholic community held by members of the reserve. Thus hostility from within the police toward catholic recruitment is also mirrored by a perceived hostility by the catholic community as a whole, toward the security forces. Membership of the RUC reserve therefore appears a much more difficult process for the catholic recruit who when joining the part time police has to detach him or herself more fully from the community than does the protestant recruit.

I originally joined back in 1972 at a time when I was 22 years old, a catholic who had seen all the various bits and pieces going on, I was working for the government at the time, I grew up in a predominantly protestant area and felt all along I needed to be doing something or should be doing something and show that as a catholic I was not afraid to do something like that. I considered the idea of joining the UDR or the RUC reserve and eventually decided on the RUC, well, I approached my parents about that at the time, they were very much against it, they thought it was far too dangerous and that there was no need as such for me to get involved in it, but I went ahead against their will and joined. (Belfast reservist)

The occupational culture of the RUC reserve may therefore ensure that catholic recruitment is limited to those who are prepared to subscribe to a set of values often apparently irreconcilable with those of the catholic community at large. The part time catholic recruit also often faces the additional problem of living and working within a community, elements of which may directly oppose part time membership. This is compounded by a general view held by the part time police that the catholic population, hostile to the police, would oppose any member of the catholic community joining the force:

... I find it rather difficult to understand exactly why few join, certainly some of the areas in which they would live ... in an area where the catholic ethos as such is built into them very much any idea of a member of their family joining the police is purely unethical to them, they wouldn't like the idea at all. (Border reservist)

... There are some catholics on the force, they can't go to their own homes, you know its not the RUC or the UDR stopping them, its their own communities and then there are shouting politicians saying there's not enough catholic members. (Belfast reservist)

... Well, they don't join round here because they would be shot as traitors, but I don't know about other parts. (Border reservist)

31

... Well, didn't you get so called politicians standing up a lot of years ago and telling catholics under no circumstances should they join the RUC or army and a month later they stand up and say its sectarian because there is very few catholics in it, I think its all politics. (Country reservist)

Chapter one described a society where the notions of community and neighbourhood are often intertwined with religion. Such community isolation may therefore reinforce attitudes of hostility toward the catholic community. These attitudes become reinforced by a recruitment process that relies heavily upon the influence of neighbourhood, family colleagues and friends. The attitudes acquired in the home and community therefore become perpetuated within the reserve. Table 2.3 demonstrates that there are few variations between the sexes in the method of initial contact and recruitment to the RUC reserve:

Table 2.3
Method of recruitment to the part time RUC

	Total %
Via the media	41
Via work colleagues	16
Via neighbours	6
Via family	24
Via friends	13

For both sexes informal contact is by far the most important recruitment medium for the organisation. Almost 30 per cent of the recruits for example, are attracted to police work by friendships developed either at their main work or outside work. There appears little variation in this recruitment method between areas, with border areas being only marginally less responsive to advertising than other areas.

The table illustrates the importance of friendships and neighbourhood as recruiting influences. Membership of the security forces may be seen as tangible evidence of community identity. It marks out the individuals' identification with the values often associated with the protestant community. Community for reservists in the country and border areas is

32

often about the physical geography of the area. The need to protect a land heritage, farms and property. The urban reservist may use the concept of community identity in terms of upholding a set of values and traditions. This process may be a choice between a number of organisations, where the RUC reserve is weighed alongside the para military UDA or UVF:

... I live on a farm and I would say this is a part of the world where most people are in the police or UDR, being a member of the RUC I suppose its all about land really, farms. I live in a very remote part of the country, about five miles from the border. As a matter of fact, I was attacked just about five years ago coming off duty! I didn't really say its me they're after, its the land you see. I would say it would cause quite a bit of annoyance to the family being in it but now that I am I don't think I would be interested in leaving it. (Border reservist)

... Well, I come from a loyalist area, although my family are not loyalists in the sense that you had it drummed into you, my father was a member of the B Specials in fact I think it was the C Specials and stationed in Londonderry round about 1922 ... What I really think happened was I tried to prove I was as good a man as what my father was, he was in the police and I wasn't and that was always in the back of my mind, so as I say I lived in a loyalist area. Most other people I knew around me all joined the UDA instead and luckily enough I stayed out of it, because there was a pressure on you to join. I joined the police and I've been in the police for 11 years. (Belfast reservist)

... There's a second motive, there was 17 of us in the Boys Brigade, we ran about together and lived in the same area, and of 17 there was only two didn't join the police force, myself and another chap who is now a minister, but in a sense I was left out because all of that group had joined the police. (Belfast reservist)

... Well, I joined the part time reserve in 1977, 18 years old at the time, I was born and raised in the Shankhill Road area and it was a case of either you were on the paramilitary side or you were on the law and order side. All my friends went the other way and I decided that wasn't for me, so I joined the RUC reserve as a way of doing my bit as I seen it at the time. I'm not quite sure what it all meant at that time at 18, but that's the way I saw it and I applied and was accepted. The decision was that at school there were forms going round to join the UDA and UVF and I didn't want to be involved in that at all. A lot of my friends did and they are serving jail sentences because of it, in the area I grew up in there were only two ways you could go, this way or the other. (Belfast reservist)

The notions of public duty and a sense of commitment to the state and its law and order lie at the root of membership of the RUC reserve. These are not politically neutral values but declare in their professing, a commitment to the principles of unionism. Union of the state of Northern Ireland with a legal structure and structure of authority and power embedded within the United Kingdom. Reserves talked about their principle reasons for joining the RUC on a part time basis. Overwhelmingly respondents in all locations and of both sexes, identify this sense of public duty as the most important reason for joining the RUC. This was far in excess of other reported reasons for joining:

Table 2.4
Motives for membership of the part time RUC

	Male %	Female %
Variety of work	16	26
Pay	5	1
Companionship	2	2
Working conditions	1	1
Public service	76	70

… The reason I joined was I thought that I'd be doing some good to the country, assisting the RUC in the normal role of duty. But, as time goes on I don't know really whether I was wise in joining up the way things have turned out over the years. (Belfast reservist)

… Well, I joined in 1972, I had two very young kids then. I joined partly for money but mainly because there was so much violence going on, I mean, the other night we were here two or three people got killed particularly in Belfast and things were much worse then than they are now. I think the best way of trying to use my spare

34

time is to try and help out. Since then its developed into liking the station I work in and I have always liked the people I worked with. (Belfast reservist)

... There are a lot of people I've been talking to who said the same thing. You'd go in, do your bit for three or four years and by that time the problem would be all over and you could go back living a normal life, but it wasn't like that! I suppose nobody really knew it would have lasted so long as it has and there's no sign of it ending, is there? (Country reservist)

... I've 15 years done and I joined out of loyalty to the country at the start but I wouldn't say that now. Well, I'm 15 years on it, 15 years past and like everyone else I joined at the time because a lot of people were doing it and thought I could do some good. I thought I would have been doing more. They wait till something happens and then the place is swarming with policemen and detectives and basically we should be able to go round and prevent things happening. (Belfast reservist)

The influence of previous policing experience in the province remains an important factor when considering contemporary attitudes. Many who join the part time RUC follow a family tradition of part time police work. Eighteen per cent of all respondents had fathers with previous part time policing experience in Northern Ireland. This tradition is most pronounced in the border areas.

Table 2.5
Respondents with fathers who had
part time police experience

	%
Belfast	14
Border	33
Country	19

Table 2.5 shows that 33 per cent of those part time police in border stations have fathers with previous part time police experience. This

35

contrasts with only 14 per cent of respondents in Belfast, whose fathers had undertaken part time duties.

The part time RUC reserve also provides an important staging post for many on their way to full time careers in the RUC. This is particularly so for women officers, over 70 per cent of whom had applied to the full time force. Part time membership may be used by the individual and the organisation as a means of gauging suitability for the job.

Table 2.6
Applications to join the full time RUC

	Belfast	Border	Country
Number	319	63	194
%	68	50	65

Table 2.6 shows that a very high proportion (almost 70 per cent overall) of the part time police had applied at some time to join the full time force. The evidence that part time police experience is being used as a stepping stone to full time employment in the RUC is not as significant in the border areas. The shows that only 50 per cent of respondents in border stations have considered applying to the full time RUC:

> I have toyed with the idea. I gave it serious consideration in 1975 and there were three of us part time in the station and the other part timer, he joined full time at that stage and there were numerous discussions about it and eventually we decided to go ahead but his idea was that within three years he was going to do his sergeant's exam and he did exactly that, and he is an inspector now and has been for quite a while. I thought about it and weighed it all up but in the end they didn't want me full time ... (Country reservist)

> Not in this last while, but over the years there has been quite a number of young men step forward and they have recruited into the regular force, say after 14 or 18 months, so it has been a recruiting ground over the years, it means that they are going in already knowing what its like on the streets ... (Belfast reservist)

> The bulk of part timers I see coming in here are all testing the water and have been encouraged to join by the recruiting branch to test the

water first and indeed the full time reserve is the same, they are being encouraged by the recruiting branch with them saying they will take them into the force in 18 months or two years. I think its a good idea. (Belfast reservist)

Those that do not move directly into full time service, form part of a tradition of long service within the part time RUC. Almost 60 per cent of respondents across all three areas had 10 or more years service with the force. This wealth of policing experience is most remarkable in the border areas with three quarters of the part time police in this area having more than ten years service. Table 2.7 shows that only eight per cent of border respondents have been recruited in the last three years. Most part time police in these border stations are older than their fellow part time police in other areas and possess more years policing experience than their city or country counterparts:

Table 2.7
Years of part time RUC service

	Belfast %	Border %	Country %
Up to 3 years service	26	8	27
With 10+ years service	55	75	49

Women tend to be the more recent recruits to part time policing. Among officers with up to three years experience in the part time police their are almost equal numbers of males and females, but women are significantly under represented among those with over 10 years of police experience.

Conclusion

The chapter has shown how the Ulster Service Corps in the form of the B Specials existed as an active part of the country's security from the 1920s. It was a force that was intertwined with the Ulster protestant ascendancy, and it served to support and reinforce a power structure notable for its exclusion of the catholic population. The B Specials were therefore one of the first important casualties of the police restructuring that followed the riots of 1969. The new reserve police force was intended to have broad cross community support and to limit its functions to supporting the full time police in their normal policing tasks.

The chapter suggests that the new RUC reserve inherited many of the attitudes and values of its predecessor. It continued a cultural milieu that remains wary of the catholic population. The chapter confirms the membership of the RUC reserve as a religiously and socially isolate group. It conforms in general to the picture of Northern Ireland provided by national research data which shows residential segregation as a major factor in attitudinal formation. The chapter suggests that there are a number of differences between those reservists who work along the border and those with an urban background. Border reservists are an older grouping with an attitude toward their policing role which may be more readily recognisable as following a tradition inherited from the former B Specials. Reservists from the city of Belfast appear more pragmatic in their approach toward policing and their reasons for part time membership. It is possible that the attitudes of officers may be influenced by length of service. It may be that younger officers entering part time service are more temperate in their views. Such a socializing process however offers no direct challenge to the distorted nature of the recruitment to the reserves which may effectively confine recruitment to members of the protestant community.

Chapter one described the sense of alienation that pervades many protestant communities. This is an alienation that arises from protestant economic and political decline. It is an alienation that may serve to reinforce traditional community values and folk memories. It may reinforce rather than erode, feelings of hostility toward the catholic community. In such a context the process of policing can be seen primarily in terms of containment of a hostile catholic population. It is important to examine whether these attitudes translate themselves into the daily policing functions of the reserve. Chapter three therefore examines the attitudes toward police work and its rewards that are held by members of the RUC reserve.

References

Cameron Commission, (1969), *Disturbances in Northern Ireland*, Cmnd. 532, Belfast HMSO.

Farrell, P. (1971), *Ireland's English question*, Batsford.

Hezlet, B. (1972), *Fermanagh B Specials*, London, Tom Stacey.

Hunt Committee. (1969), *Report of the advisory committee on police in Northern Ireland*, Cmnd. 535, Belfast HMSO.

Oliver, J. (1978), *Working at Stormont*, Institute of public administration.

Scarman Tribunal. (1969), *Report of the tribunal of inquiry into violence and civil disturbances in Northern Ireland*, Vol. 1, and 2. Cmnd. 566, Belfast HMSO.

Tierney, M. (1978), *Modern Ireland*, Gill and Macmillan.

3 Police work

Introduction

The history of the part time RUC reserve, reinforced by the religious composition of its current membership suggests a group of police whose behaviours remain rooted in the orthodoxies of traditional policing in Northern Ireland, and who view policing primarily in terms of accommodating a catholic community perceived as fundamentally hostile to the state. This chapter therefore explores these views in the context of the part time policing of Northern Ireland. It looks at the level of commitment required from part time officers, and the financial rewards inherent in part time policing. It highlights the attitudes of part time officers toward their full time colleagues and looks at the specific policing tasks required of part time officers and the satisfaction that is gained from this employment. It also explores the particular problems faced by women part time officers within the RUC, and the attitudes of women toward the carrying of weapons.

The part time RUC reserve does not fit easily into the literature concerning volunteer policing in the rest of the United Kingdom. Leon (1989) notes that there have been volunteer special constables in England and Wales since the Special Constables Act 1831. There has been recent renewed interest in the role of the special constables. This interest arises from spiralling police manpower costs, and government promotion of the concept of the "active citizen". Special constables account for about 11 per cent of total police manpower in Great Britain and are now viewed as a perfect vehicle for providing a supportive link between the regular constabulary and the community. They are unpaid volunteers and work an average of three hours per week. Special constables have their own organizational hierarchy and there is considerable variation between police authorities in the use and deployment of special constables. However the report of the Police Advisory Board (1981) noted that there is a traditional friction between these part time volunteers and regular police who may consider that the volunteers undermine the potential for overtime pay since they remain a very cheap manpower source for police authorities.

The part time RUC reserve bears little similarity to the special constabularies of England, Scotland and Wales. It is a paid, and a single rank element of the police structure in Northern Ireland. It is built upon a long foundation of community involvement in the defence of the province from terrorism. Similarly throughout Britain there is not a pattern of social segregation and police organisation that is evident in Northern Ireland. The membership of the part time RUC reserve is made up of those wishing to preserve a political union and to counter the challenge of republicanism. Chapter two suggests that this founding principle still provides a major factor in the current membership attitudes of the RUC reserve. The RUC reserve today, still plays a role in a society which was established and maintained on the basis of an ethnic and political domination. It is this historic interrelationship of the RUC reserve with the protestant unionist power structure that sets it apart from the special constabularies in the rest of the United Kingdom.

Pay and commitment

Chapter two suggested that the notions of public duty and a sense of commitment to the state and its law and order lie at the root of membership of the RUC reserve. It is particularly interesting to note the low positions given to pay and conditions as the primary reason for joining. It might have been expected that younger part time police, or those with specific financial needs would give pay as the main reason for taking up a second job. In reality few give pay as a primary reason, thus the ideas of commitment and public duty transcend all other issues to form the foundations of membership.

Looking however exclusively at the principle reason for joining the RUC may not give a wholly accurate picture of true motivation. Pay emerges more strongly as secondary and third considerations for membership of the part time police:

Table 3.1
Age of part time officers and pay
as a reason for joining

	Age -29	Age 30-39	Age 40-49	Age 50+
Pay first reason %	4	4	3	3
Pay second reason %	8	12	12	9
Pay third reason %	30	24	20	18

Table 3.1 shows that pay is an important second or third consideration for joining. Pay is clearly an important reason for being in the reserves among those aged under 40 years. Thus for example 30 per cent of those police aged under 30 give pay as the third most important reason for joining the RUC. This contrasts with only 18 per cent of those aged over 50 years. Attitudes toward pay are also influenced by location:

Table 3.2
Location of part time officers
and pay as a reason for joining

	Belfast	Border	Country
Pay first reason %	4	3	2
Pay second reason %	13	8	9
Pay third reason %	27	16	19

The importance of pay as an additional reason for joining differs by region with the highest levels of instrumental motivation being in Belfast: 44 per cent of part time officers in Belfast rank pay as one of the three most important reasons for joining the part time police, compared with 30 per cent and 27 per cent in country and border regions respectively. Border respondents tend also to be an older grouping and were often quite clear about the part played by money in their decision to join:

> ... The time I joined most of us were still doing our driving tests, the police were putting us through our driving test and I wasn't interested

in driving police cars but they put everybody in for it... I went out into the motor. I got in and it was "buck leppin'" a wee bit and the officer didn't pass me anyway; but he asked me "what did I join the part timers for, for the money or what?" and I says to myself "well, maybe you're a right smart ass, but I got my cheque anyway that day and it was 87p, and so I went down and I says, "I want to show you my cheque, 87p, and says I, I joined it for the money, and he said, "I'm sorry"! (Border reservist)

... In the special constabulary (B Specials) you got £15 per annum, no matter how many duties you did and it was a matter of ringing them up and saying you needed them to do an extra duty and it was no problem, they came in even though they know they weren't getting paid for it. I think that's the problem now with the part time reserve, it is too well paid. I think its attracting an element now that they are only there for the money. (Border reservist)

... Well, its not the most important thing to me, I have a fairly good job so the money I don't think is great. I've done it for love, and walked for four full hours for three and a tanner an hour, so if that's not love I don't know what is! (Border reservist)

Motives of social commitment are therefore intertwined with those of financial reward. Take home pay represents a significant reason for membership of the part time RUC reserve particularly among those younger reservists, and those working in the urban setting of Belfast.

Table 3.3 shows that the modal income group for part time duty is within the range £141-£200 per month. There are however, slight differences in earnings between the sexes at the monthly income extremes. Thus 11 per cent of females earn under £80 per month from part time police work, compared to only 6 per cent of males. However almost 9 per cent of male respondents earn over £240 per month from police duties, compared to 5 per cent of females. Earnings are higher on average in border and country areas than in Belfast. Over half the respondents from border and country stations earned more than £140 per month, compared to 41 per cent of Belfast reservists:

Table 3.3
Monthly earnings of part time officers

	Belfast %	Border %	Country %
Earnings under £80	10	7	3
Earnings £81-£120	36	21	25
Earnings £121-£140	13	18	15
Earnings £141-£200	29	29	35
Earnings £201-£240	8	14	12
Earnings over £241	4	10	10

Pay of course reflects the number of hours that are worked. The longest hours are worked by part time police in border stations. Table 3.5 shows that Belfast stations have the highest proportion; that is one third; of part time police who are working less than six hours per week. By contrast one third of those in border stations devote more than 10 hours per week to policing duties:

Table 3.4
Hours of police work of part time officers

	Belfast %	Border %	Country %
Up to 6 hours per week	33	14	18
6-10 hours per week	51	52	54
Over 10 hours per week	16	33	26

The number of hours available for policing may be a function both of the demands of the force and the availability of the part time officer. However although respondents provided information on the hours worked in their full time employment,there is no clear relationship between working few hours in full time employment and devoting more hours to the RUC. This may suggest that hours of work for the part time RUC are dictated by the force itself and provide little opportunity for individual manipulation.

The payment of part time police officers and the hours of work required of them may be determining factors in the crucial relationship between the part time officers and their full time colleagues. Part time officers expressed considerable concern at the nature of this relationship. The nature of policing in Northern Ireland places great demands on the force's manpower, with considerable opportunities for overtime available to full time officers. This may serve to ameliorate the relationship between the full and part time officers. However the relatively high levels of full time police pay are seen by many part time officers as sometimes undermining the full time officers' effectiveness in policing:

> Well, in my opinion it comes down to one thing, money to a young policeman. I think its very hard for a fellah of 18 or 19 to get an £1,800 or £1,900 a month of wages and go out and talk to the like of my father who worked most of his life in Shorts for £100 a week, and I'm actually a public servant, so they go out with the attitude, "look at me, I've £1,800 a month and a new XR3, this man here he's only got £100 a week, who's he? - why should I have to call him sir, I've more money than he has". Its immaturity, I think. (Belfast reservist)

> I don't know the reason for all the regulars joining but some have joined maybe because of the money and in it for the money. They get their hours and overtime done but they're not really interested in people. They end up with a lot of money, but there is not the commitment that there used to be when maybe the pay was less. (Border reservist)

Part time officers may therefore regard high pay for full time officers as a major factor in isolating the full time officer from the traditional values that are held by the part time officer. Full time officers are seen as holding an overwhelmingly instrumental attitude toward policing. This may run counter to many part time officers whose view of policing is coloured by an occupational culture committed to a particular anti nationalist perspective. There is a general recognition among part time officers that they derive their policing skills from their experience of full time employment, living and working within the wider community. It is the essential part time nature of their policing which it is argued distinguishes the part time officer from the full time officer:

We are good on patrol because we are dealing with the public in our own civilian jobs, but an ordinary policeman, he puts on a uniform and he's automatically a law enforcer and I think he gets a bit big headed about it at times. I think he would socialize more within the force than the reserve would. He's always looking for a "baddy" we're not always looking for them, we are mixing with the general public in our own job, you are getting their views as well, but the majority of a policeman's views are wrong ones, he's dealing with culprits. (Belfast reservist)

A lot of people who have gone to the regular police from school have never been used to working with ordinary civilians whereas a part time member is doing a job and used to dealing with the public. If you did work in an atmosphere it means you understand how the ordinary person lives and how he has to cope with life but if you leave school or college and go into the police you are sort of brainwashed if that's a right word or a bad word to say, you are trained in one thing, but you forget how the other half lives ... (Country reservist)

Our role has changed, we were more inclined to deal with things we found on the ground in our own way, but now we are a back up to the regulars ... In the past we'd find an accident, find a drunk driving a car and we would have taken a different approach to it depending on who the person was. A regular mind you would just go straight in without thinking who the person is. (Country reservist)

This may be described as a clash between tradition and modernity. It is a clash between those who may use a discretionary judgement based on experience accumulated and reinforced within the wider realms of full time work and community, and those whose discretionary judgement may derive almost exclusively from the experience of policing itself. This distinction may lie at the root of many of the tensions that exist in the operational relationship between full and part time officers. Numerous accounts were volunteered of part time skills being ignored or causing friction with full time colleagues. This is particularly the case of reservists working in Belfast. It may be that the nature of the relationship differs between Belfast and rural areas. In rural areas, particularly toward the border, full time officers may commute in from safer areas, and come to rely more heavily upon the knowledge the part time officer has of the area in which he lives and works. The policing skills that are held by the part time officer in border areas may therefore be held in higher regard by full time colleagues, than those skills held by part time officers in Belfast:

> The problem is that the regulars would never let you interfere, it would be looked on very badly. Because you're a part time man, we have no say. Well, I interfered once and it took months to out live it. In the occasion I'm talking about the person grossly overstepped what he was doing and I told him so and for months I had terrible trouble from him. (Belfast reservist)

> If you do work in industry at all, you are meeting and working with people so you can talk to people better than an ordinary policeman from the department who has no experience whatsoever. He jumps in with both feet and creates a situation many a time when there's no situation there at all. The young police coming in now have a bad or wrong attitude than other people that come in, if they stop cars or people in the street, some of them, not them all, do have a problem, and say "I am the police, so you'll do as I say and answer what I ask you or I'll march you down to the barracks and you can tell me there". A lot of them do that, but us being part time cannot interfere and say "don't say that". (Belfast reservist)

> If a young policeman comes in from 18, all he knows is police really, he doesn't know anything about life, he's coming straight from school and going into the police, yes, some of them, they know their job but do they really have any feelings when they go to a family row or are they just sorting it out? Where we would go and try and listen and comfort a bit more because we have more time. They're not interested in that and we get told to stay outside and keep out of it. (Belfast reservist)

> We have gone out on patrol, two or three reserve boys in a landrover and after two or three nights you got to know all the regulars and they found out you were a person that you could move your lips and such(!) and then you were just one of the boys. But if he's not the type of person to start a conversation he'll walk past you, you never mix so there is no comradeship. (Belfast reservist)

> I have seen it happen, getting young lads, who were to me causing no offence to anyone, in an area, peaceful area and situation, middle of the day, and the police arriving and jumping out of the vehicle

stopping these lads, spreading them against the railings of a school, and searching them and giving them some hassle and I couldn't see any reason for it and I would agree on a couple of occasions the police have been harsh with young people, but I wouldn't say a thing at the time, I would be told to mind my own business, I mean you have to work with people ... (Belfast reservist)

Part time duties

Part time policing in Northern Ireland involves two principal types of duty; patrolling and static guard duty. Patrol activity may perform the functions of reassurance to the local community, to deter terrorist activity, or to fulfil a particular policing function such as the service of a summons. In many instances the patrol may have military support. Patrolling may in many cases take place in police landrovers although in some areas such a form of mobility may be considered too vulnerable to attack. Guard duty is a necessary condition of policing in Northern Ireland. The police station itself may prove an attractive static target to terrorist attack. The duty of guarding the station may be achieved with relatively limited training, may require limited agility and is a task readily allocated to part time officers. Discussions with part time police have suggested a general decline in the role of the part time force and a shift in the work of the part time police, away from patrolling toward more static duties, although it would be unclear whether this demonstrated a general trend:

> Yeah, years ago they used to take regular men off the streets when there was any trouble and left the reserve on the street but the attitude was - you live among these people and you know them and they'll not bother you. They were calling you in from your own work years ago, now some of the comments are - are you in tonight again taking our overtime! (Belfast reservist)

> ... About half station security and half patrolling the general area, but that duty has changed a lot over the years, initially when I joined I had 8 or 10 beats in a sub division so you were generally doing duty on a two or three man beat patrol, then as time went on, we had more station security duties. I would have to say its a change for the worse, I prefer the beat patrol and being in contact with the public more. (Country reservist)

It has changed. It has changed more or less overall, I think. Its hard to read somebody else's mind, but everybody knows that there are far more regulars than full time reserves than there was 15 years ago. Whenever I joined here there was about four in a section and that was it, and there was the army and the UDR doing security here two thirds of the time. When we started here at the beginning we would have been here everyday of the week, now if you get in once, well, that's really good enough. There was a time when there were 12 to 15 part timers here and they have all fallen by the wayside. (Border reservist)

There are also significant regional differences in the deployment of part time officers. The border stations, although generally composed of older part time police, devote considerably more of their time to patrolling than other activities; 74 per cent of border reservists spend most of their time on mobile patrols. This contrasts with fewer than 50 per cent of Belfast respondents, most of whom would spend their time on static guard duty. This high incidence of patrolling in the border stations is not readily explicable. It could be however that in border stations there may be a higher turnover of full time police who live outside the area. In this instance the part time police may be fulfilling their original role of providing local knowledge and geography in their patrolling activity with their full time colleagues.

It is however within the border stations that the feelings of decline in the role and significance of the part time force are most acutely felt. Thus despite the importance of the part time role in border stations there is a general concern at the marginalization of the part time force:

Well, they had an advert in the paper about a year ago and they were looking for them round Bangor and places like that. There was a young fellah down near me, applied to join and it cost more to protect him that the whole exercise was worth ... I don't really think they want you in this division. Not in this division at all ... But he got into the UDR no problem at all. The last man who joined here was over three years ago. They are winding down the part timers in these sort of exposed areas, I mean, you can get as many part timers as you want in Bangor but its not exactly achieving anything. Its the same in Ballymena and those places, there's hundreds. I think it is depressing because there are so many outsiders that they never really get to know the area or the people, there's very few that come down have been here any length of time. We go into meetings in Newry the odd time with the bosses and they say, "oh, your doing a great job and we don't know what we'd do without you", but that's only a lot of old bluff. (Border reservist)

The instructions are "don't recruit them if you can't protect them", so they're not encouraging them to recruit really. Really the fellahs in the dangerous areas are more keen to join than the fellahs in the safe areas. But the ones in dangerous areas they wouldn't take them on unless full time. We had 20 part timers at one time. We now have 10 and there's nobody joining. Some have been intimidated out, some have been killed, my sections down to two. (Border reservist)

Guard duty is a generally unpopular activity. Reservists were asked to rank their preferred duties on preference scale of 1-5. Table 3.5 suggests that only 17 per cent of males would regard it as their preferred work option:

Table 3.5
Guard duties as a preferred duty

	Male %	Female %
First preference	17	4
Second preference	14	8
Third preference	32	12
Fourth preference	30	51
Fifth preference	7	25

The preference for guard duty is related to age; the older part time police are more attracted to static guard duty than their younger counterparts, with nearly half (48 per cent) of those who ranked guard duty as their first or second preference aged more than 45 years:

Well, I do mostly guard duty to be honest with you, but if they are short of drivers I would generally be asked to drive the police cars. I prefer the guard duties at my age, I work the 10 hours, you can sit down and watch the TV and rest yourself because its tiresome, when you are driving an armoured police van, its over a ton weight, its very strenuous on the arms and your looking out two different screens, you can't see where you are going, it may be raining as well, and it can be pretty tense. Then of course, your areas restricted where you are driving as well, your out of bounds here and out of bounds there, your driving around the same bloody roads so many times a night, so the guard duty is handy, you can sit and listen to the radio. (Belfast reservist)

Well, the station I'm attached to, the duties are usually two hours security and two hours patrolling, during patrol time you're out in all weathers assisting in road stops and your other two hours are security. I prefer security. I think its a lot safer. I'm sitting there in a hut that's surrounded by all these five or six monitors across the front wall and you have heating. (Country reservist)

There is however a general recognition that the changing nature of the terrorist threat has forced an operational change upon the part time reserve. The threat to stations is considered such that a considerable amount of manpower is necessarily committed to station security:

I would say what has been said in banter around the station that we are perhaps the highest paid car park attendants in Belfast. The situation has changed in the city this while back as far as security is concerned as they bombed Chichester Street and round there so we now have to have a number of security points to cover 24 hours a day. Our role is to assist the full time, and it doesn't cause me any great difficulty, because we are only going out there for four hours to relieve a person who has been there all day so I don't mind, its not every single night you are doing that. Last Friday night for instance we were out on the beat up in the city centre and we were doing things. (Belfast reservist)

The policing in and around the town has changed so much its a bonus to see a policeman on the street at night time and I think its very sad in that we are all more or less confined to a high percentage of security duties and there is so little action for the "bobby on the beat" which the public want to see. (Country reservist)

Patrolling remains the universally preferred form of part time police activity. An average 73 per cent of male and female part time police ranked either mobile or beat patrolling as their first or second preferred duty. Patrolling is an activity that is universally popular irrespective of region:

Table 3.6
Patrol duty as a preferred duty

	Belfast %	Border %	Country %
Mobile patrol first or second preference	68	82	78
Beat patrol first or second preference	80	73	73

It is the particular skills of patrolling a local area that are regarded highly by part time officers. It is the ability to know a particular area, its characters and its geography that part time officers often consider are skills which they derive from both living and working in the area. This may place them apart from the full time officer who may commute to work and spend a limited time posted to a particular station:

> If you are not doing something like patrolling you lose touch, especially with the community in and around this area. I think its bad for community relations because the good side of the community, the normal law abiding citizen isn't seeing where their tax money is going to. I think it has been a policy decision possibly for our own safety that you are not exposed as much. (Country reservist)

> The patrolling is the best part of it and that's where you got most of your information through stopping at somebody's door walking down Sandy Row or Donegall Road and having a yarn. She would maybe drop something that you were able to build up on but now when nobody is out on foot you don't get any information unless somebody rings in, and you don't get that very often. (Belfast reservist)

> Years back the part timers were always out and then we were being mobile, it depended on the sergeant. If he wants to know the country he gets a part timer out who knows the ground and the houses and

52

people, and other sergeant's want you on security and that's it. (Country reservist)

Patrolling represents the public face of the RUC reserve. It is a police function at the interface of communities. The function of patrolling may be to deter crime and reassure the community by the police presence. The attitudes of the reservist toward the community being policed are therefore central to the success of that patrolling function. It is important therefore to understand how the protestant nature of the force and its attendant attitudes and history, translate themselves into the behaviour of officers. It is evident that the officers themselves recognize the divided nature of the areas which they may police, and their place within that social division:

If you want to put it into religion, most of the part time men are all protestant and all stick to protestant pubs and don't mix at all. You can't go into a roman catholic pub - you would be asked to leave, we are segregated that way, but its not of your choice, its really a fact of life. You wouldn't feel safe and before the night would be out you would possibly be picked on anyway. What they would say is "what the hell is he doing in here anyway, is he looking for information", so its your choice. Well, really you never think, "I'll not go into a roman catholic pub, I'll go into a protestant pub", you just automatically go to your local where you can sit and relax and have a decent drink. You never think in your mind its a protestant pub or a roman catholic pub. (Border reservist)

You can distinguish your own kind. You can sort of know who is genuine and who is not. (Country reservist)

Any catholics I know I get on with OK, it doesn't make any difference, eh, I don't know how you would change the situation to bring them together, they are separated from schooling, from birth, and depends where you are born and who you live beside whether you mix or not. (Belfast reservist)

The nature of the organisational culture of the part time reserve necessarily affects the manner of policing and relations with the catholic community, and the perceptions of the RUC that are held by the catholic community. This was dramatically illustrated by a number of officers:

It has to be said, we are seen by some as a protestant force yes, if you are in the middle of Duncairn Gardens (an interface area) you may or may not work in that area if the winds blowing right you will get battered from one side or shot from the other, but you know yourself what to expect, you can still speak to people in that area mainly on the protestant side, but there's very few you can speak to on this side of the barriers. (Belfast reservist)

There would be a certain amount of basis for it (discrimination) in certain cases, I'm sure, and with certain individuals, men wouldn't have the right way of approaching the public, or the right way of approaching the man they stop and things may get out of hand, but in no way is it general, its very isolated. In our area we rarely have any complications at all. (Country reservist)

The absence of any meaningful involvement with the catholic community, and the almost total absence of catholic members of the force affects the nature of police operations. Isolation from the community constrains the police to operating on the margins of the community, often stopping and checking those entering or leaving the area. There is therefore some recognition that the nature of policing requires the police to have a higher profile in catholic areas which may militate against community support:

Its very seldom you would get any hassle, I think the substance comes from the fact that there are probably more road blocks in catholic areas than there are in protestant areas, for the simple fact that is where a lot of the main trouble has tended to arise. You have to react to this and there's no point putting up a road block in Saintfield every five minutes of the day, because its a peaceful community and long may it continue to be so. (Belfast reservist)

I mean, I can see in some places if I came from certain places around Northern Ireland, I would not be keen on the police or the UDR. But I can travel around, in and out of work, and once in a blue moon be stopped by police or a patrol but I know if I go across the bridge to the far side of the city, I could get stopped at every street corner and it can be a nuisance there's no question about it and it would get my back up in ordinary circumstances even if you weren't that way inclined. (Belfast reservist)

You can't say if ones are better than others, you can speak to them and try and be friendly with them, but after that you don't know. I do know a man who actually said to me, he lives up in the "Park" area and he said its no wonder people are getting involved because every time he comes out he's stopped and searched by the army and he said he wasn't involved in anything but he said that would make people get involved. Well, I don't see what you can do about it. I don't know. (Country reservist)

People that live in areas we term as not good areas want to get on with their lives and you find when you do keep stopping them the biggest majority understand that, because of where they live and if they're the decent ordinary person they don't feel harassed, they understand that that's part of the territory they come from. (Country reservist)

The tasks required of the police may therefore run counter to the objective of widespread community acceptance. It may be that it is the interface nature of patrolling that makes it so popular among many part time officers. Patrolling may be seen as the "battleground" between the communities where the officer's perceptions of the minority community are tested in the public domain. Patrolling for part time police, remains the most popular of police activities and provides the greatest levels of satisfaction. It is possible to construct a measure of the satisfaction which part time police have in the duties which they perform. This measure is achieved by looking at those who, in ranking their preferred police duties, ranked as their first choice that activity on which they spend most of their police time:

Table 3.7
Part time police and satisfaction
with their primary activity

Type of duty	Belfast % Giving 1st preference	Border % Giving 1st preference	Country % Giving 1st preference
Guard	26	59	29
Patrol	59	74	61
Desk	5	50	33
Other	47	25	20

Table 3.7 shows that only 29 per cent of those who spend their time mostly doing guard duty, gave this as their preferred form of policing activity. The table confirms the attractions of patrolling for part time police. Over 60 per cent of those who rank patrolling as their preferred activity actually spend their time engaged in patrolling. This preference and work pattern may be further analyzed by region, since the pattern of working may vary between regions. It emerges that those working in border stations appear to be a more content part time force, since a higher proportion are doing those jobs that they wish to do.

The general impression is of relatively high levels of job satisfaction amongst part time police officers. This is a satisfaction born directly from the civil conflict. It is a satisfaction that derives from commitment to a cause,or from having saved life or averted disaster:

> I think its a very dull, boring job, with long hours of complete boredom - underneath there is always a possibility and a fear, that always is there even though you try to ignore it. You get your uniform on, go into the parade room where you're detailed by the sergeant, you near enough know what you are going to do because there are so few people turned up you are either on the front or back gate. I have always said to myself, at least your doing something! (Country reservist)

> Well, I think of the part time policewoman killed in Bangor and it was a Sunday evening and she was walking up High Street with another constable and it was a freak thing that there was a bomb planted but it was actually her radio that killed her, the pressure of it, she was married with two children which I had at the time, and wasn't all that long in the job at the time. It was terrible, its something you don't forget about, but it made all the work I've done worthwhile. (Country reservist)

> Well, its the hope that someday something maybe done to get the issue solved and I can say, "well, I helped do that", or if the worst possible situation comes, that I will be there to assist" ... you are doing something and you will never let terrorism win even though everybody will admit we're doing very little, you keep on doing it. (Country reservist)

Female employment

The critical problems that face women officers within police forces in general, find a strong echo among female part time officers within the RUC. Women in the force are confronted by an occupational role that is culturally ascribed. Thus women officers may find themselves concentrated in the traditional support roles rather than line activities:

Table 3.8
The work of part time officers

Main task	Male %	Female %
Guard	46	5
Mobile/beat patrolling	52	64
Desk reception	0	21
Other	2	10

Table 3.8 shows that almost half of the male respondents reported that their primary activity was static guard duty, but this applied to a very small proportion of female respondents. Moreover the nature of the guard duty differs since female constables may be primarily concerned to guard individual female prisoners whilst their male counterparts will be concerned with base security. Female officers are more likely to spend their duty hours in an interface with the public. Women are also much more likely to spend time on desk reception activity, which did not feature as work activity among male respondents.

Bryant and Dunkerley (1985) note that the issues that surround the integration of female police officers into the general mainstream of police activity are still a matter of considerable debate. Police work is often viewed as maintaining a traditionally male image which reinforces a view that women are better suited to the more traditional types of work and lack the physical strength to do the full range of tasks. This typification of police women may be reinforced by strong sets of male attitudes and behaviours that serve to marginalize women. Most women officers spoke of this behaviour pattern within the workplace:

Well I think from the start you are more or less tried. I remember at the start the men tried to see how far they could push me and sort of slagging me all the time, but I must say the women nowadays won't leave over the head of that. They give as good as they get. It wouldn't bother them. (Country reservist)

Oh yes, you always do (get bantered) you just take it in your stride. Some women would get really annoyed but if you worry about it, your life wouldn't be worth living so to speak. (Belfast reservist)

I feel, well if you can give as good as what you are getting, it soon stops. I must admit I have never felt that it has got to the stage where this is terrible and I have to pack this in and go somewhere else, I felt I could cope alright with it and I would feel 90 per cent of the females can. This is no place for a feminist. I have noticed one or two very young part time girls coming in and I just think they test them to see if they are going to be able to stick the banter or not. I feel if they can't they just shouldn't really be there because I think you've got to make up your mind and say "right, I'm going to be working with 99 per cent male and I need to be able to cope with them". I would say if the same things were said in a different organisation such as the civil service there would be one hell of a row! It wouldn't be acceptable in most organisations. (Belfast reservist)

There are men definitely who think that you are a nuisance and that you are a liability when you are out with them, which I suppose to a certain extent is true. My husband takes notions and says I don't need to do this and wishes I would give it up but he does fully understand the situation. (Border reservist)

The problem of the occupational role confronting female officers in the RUC is compounded by the terrorist threat and the need to carry firearms. In the United Kingdom police officers do not as a rule carry firearms except for special situations. No distinction is made between males and females in this regard. Within Northern Ireland however all male officers carry firearms when performing regular duties.

The problem in Northern Ireland was graphically illustrated by the litigation in the case of Johnston v chief constable of the RUC (1980). In this case, Mrs Johnston had been employed as a member of the full time reserve on a series of three year contracts since 1974. In 1980 the chief constable of the RUC refused to renew her contract and those of her fellow female officers. This decision was taken because of a policy of not permitting women to carry firearms or participate in firearm training. This policy existed because of the need to reduce the risks of attack upon female officers. It also formed part of an overall long term aim of the chief constable to establish an unarmed force. The chief constable also argued that armed policewomen would be less effective in the roles for which they were best suited, in particular welfare work and dealing with families and children. Mrs Johnston was compelled to accept a part time post with the RUC. The position was summed up by the chief constable who explained that:

> If, in 1974 people in Northern Ireland had suddenly seen women appear carrying machine guns and batons, they would have considered those responsible to be lunatics. (Industrial tribunal)

A female superintendent argued in evidence at the tribunal that she saw the role of women in the RUC as having the opportunity of performing duty in all the specialized branches and the uniformed section. However women carrying firearms would be aggressive:

> I believe that in bearing arms we are destroying a traditional image of the welfare and preventative side of the force ... I believe women can be very effective and are doing an excellent job in the uniformed section in their restricted role. I believe that within the uniformed section the women can be very effective, I am sorry if I seem prejudiced against women.

Mrs Johnston took an action under the Northern Ireland Sex Discrimination Order 1976. After considerable litigation both within the province and at the European Court Mrs Johnston and others received substantial damages. The actions of the Chief Constable generated considerable resentment among female officers:

> We were on three yearly contracts, and in fact I was one of the lucky ones, because I still had a couple of years to go, when we found out we weren't going to be kept on. I feel very bitter about the way they treated us I do. Since the case was up, they seem to be thinking more about women than they did before. (Country reservist)

Well, I was very resentful at the time we were being discriminated against. I was determined to see it through and win our rights I was annoyed against the attitude it was such blatant discrimination against women. So as regards the arms, I also have trained in firearms, but I wouldn't personally like to have to carry a gun, but I do think women should have batons, we are used in public duty every weekend and I think we should have batons. For example the most recent was a mini riot near a restaurant in the city, and there was six of us injured all together and I was one of them, I was tramped on the ground by two screaming women and a man at the one time and you have no means of protection at all, at least the men have batons. (Belfast reservist)

Well, certainly at the time I really was very annoyed because quite often I was the only part time women here at this stage, you would get a phone call maybe at 3 am in the morning, would you mind dropping in, we have a woman prisoner, and faithfully I never refused, I got out of bed at all hours of the morning, I came in, I gave my time which I set out to do and just all of a sudden, just about within a month, they were able to switch off completely and just say, right, we don't require your services any more which was very hard to understand. I really did feel bitter about it. (Country reservist)

The chief constable's actions also divided female officers on the particular issue of carrying weapons. Many female part time officers would not welcome the requirement to carry a weapon:

I don't really think they should. If we were trained that if anything happened that we would know enough to know how to use a gun ... if we were fit to use a gun or maybe fire, at least you are going to scare them off if nothing else, so I think we should be trained and not necessarily carry. (Belfast reservist)

Well, when I was in the police originally we did do firearms training with the men and did fire weapons but I don't honestly think that I would personally want to. I think I would feel it a big responsibility - its maybe a personal thing like that. (Country reservist)

There is now a policy of sexual equality within the force. The force also agreed to reduce the height requirements for women applicants to 5'4'' from

5' 6''. It also agreed to replace the force order which restricted hours of work for part time police with an order requiring the deployment of reservists on the basis of operational needs, without reference to sex; and to provide equal access for women and men to all forms of employment opportunities. Part time female officers however still find their role often limited to those activities traditionally associated with the female officer:

> Well, seeing to female prisoners is the thing I would do that is peculiar to a women. I would do more office work than going out with patrols. I don't go out with patrols at all now. (Border reservist)

> There are certainly problems, like the time they kept saying "we've cut your hours because you can't go out and do the same work as the men are doing or we don't have the work for you because you are not armed and you can't go out and do such work as the Sangar (guard duty) because you're not armed", but I honestly feel there is enough work in the RUC for females, separate from what the males do because you are dealing with females and there always has to be a female around with another female. (Belfast reservist)

> My duties vary from STO, which is answering the phones, helping with people coming in, to duty in the landrover or in the car, because we don't carry weapons that's why we are not stuck with security duty all the time, so I get good variation which I enjoy. (Country reservist)

The majority of part time reservists appear content with the range of duties that they are required to perform. Table 3.9 shows however that there is a group of part time police which considers that the duties that they perform are "too restricting". This view differs by age with a higher proportion of younger respondents who consider their duties "too restrictive":

Table 3.9
Part time police and their duties

	Age under 34	Age 35-45	Age over 46
	%	%	%
Duties too wide	2	1	1
Duties just right	53	60	73
Duties too restrictive	45	39	26

It might have been thought that part time police in border stations would regard their role as too restrictive and feel more frustration when compared to part time police in other areas. It is the border stations that in many instances have experienced the cutting edge of terrorist activity. However 80 per cent of border part time police are satisfied with the duties that they perform, and only 17 per cent regard them as too restrictive. It may be that the age profile of part time officers in the border stations tends towards increasing the job satisfaction.

Reservists were asked whether they believed that the role of the part time RUC will change significantly over the coming years and if so, in what way? The majority believe that the role will remain much the same, but younger part time police (aged up to 29 years) are less likely to believe that the role will decrease.

Table 3.10
Future role of the part time force

	Belfast %	Border %	Country %
Role increase	22	14	18
Remain same	58	53	61
Role decrease	20	33	21

The most pessimistic views concerning the future of the part time RUC are held by those working in border stations. Table 3.10 shows that in the border stations (where part time police have experienced little recruitment to their ranks in recent years) a third of officers consider the role of their force will diminish in the future.

Conclusion

This chapter has outlined the work activities of part time reservists. It has highlighted a number of factors that distinguish part time policing in Northern Ireland from that within the rest of the United Kingdom. In Northern Ireland part time policing forms part of a complex mixture of social and political commitment. No other region within the United Kingdom faces the same sort of internal threat which demands the same levels of policing commitment. Also part time policing in Northern Ireland offers significant financial reward, elsewhere it remains unpaid volunteer effort whereas within Northern Ireland the monies earned from part time policing may form an important element of the officers' disposable income.

The chapter also notes that despite considerable advances in the role of females in the RUC, the female officer still confronts a number of problems. The RUC reserve possesses a language code that is particularly hostile toward women. Female officers remain unarmed and are consequently limited in their operational contribution.

The chapter has highlighted a number of differences in the duties of part time officers. Officers in stations along the border appear less concerned with the financial rewards of part time policing, than their urban colleagues. The chapter suggests that the nature of part time policing may be subject to change. Along the border and within many country stations the part time officer is still able to perform a traditional role of patrolling and providing to the full time police, local knowledge of the community. It appears however that within the city of Belfast and larger urban areas these traditional skills may no longer be valued. The more mobile urban communities may result in the marginalization of the part time officer relegating the officer to merely that of providing physical support to the full time officer. Those officers who work along the border appear to recognize that their role may become more limited in the future, and that the demand for these traditional part time skills of local knowledge and understanding may diminish. It is when patrolling that the stark realities of policing in Northern Ireland are confronted by the part time reservist. Many could recount horrific experiences that had clearly affected their attitude to society. These were experiences that were deeply ingrained upon memory and had often compounded hostile attitudes about the nature of the violence in Northern Ireland:

> To me it was King's Mills, that was the shooting at the protestant minibus ... the thing I remember is the lunch boxes lying with bullet holes through them, false teeth lying, the blood was running about because it was a wet night, that was January 1976 and the things still clear in my mind ... The worst thing that happened was they asked the company who they were and the protestants tried to shield the roman catholic and vice versa, but the terrorists found out which ones were the roman catholics and let them go home and opened fire on the rest of them. How could you be tolerant after that! (Border reservist)

> ... there was an almighty bang and it came over the air that there was an explosion reported in the Markets area of the city. We went round to it we were the second call sign to arrive, there were four young police officers male and a female and their armour plated landrover had been cut - the roof taken right off it and it was so sad, two had died on the spot and we help get the other three into the ambulances and it was a tragic sight, it just seemed to be a moments lapse of concentration and five lives were lost just like that. It annoyed me more to see the female young girl it really was horrific ... It brought it home to me the thin line between life and death. (Belfast reservist)

> I don't think I'll ever forget the scene when they murdered the soldiers, or either the people in Ligoneil and some of the women, because I can't justify any death, no matter where it is or who it is, what I really can't get out of my mind is those women jeering when we brought those people back down the road. Well, that incident at Ardoyne will always stick out in my mind, the attitude of the people they were first on the scene and were cheering and the ambulance arrived and the driver threw a white blanket over him and it immediately turned red and again and all these people did was jeer. (Belfast reservist)

> ... we got a call and there was a young lad had been shot outside the local pub and I got down on my knees and made him comfortable and he was shot through the head and the priest came to give him the last rights and he died in my arms he was just about the same age as my brother and I thought that could have been him. (Country reservist)

64

One evening we were called to Greencastle, a bomb had gone off in Greencastle and there was about four or five people blown to pieces and we were given plastic bags to pick up bits of people and I say every time I see that, what's going to happen to this country we live in? (Belfast reservist)

References

Leon, The Mythical history of the specials Liverpool law review, Vol. xi, (2). 89, pp. 187-197.

Police advisory board for England and Wales second working party on special constabulary, 1981.

4 The social and work life of part time police reservists

Introduction

The part time RUC reservists have been shown to be a predominantly protestant occupational group with their attitudes toward policing embedded in their accumulated experiences. These derive from history, and their perceptions of social and work life. This chapter describes the social and occupational background of part time police officers. The chapter explores the friendship and family patterns of part time officers, and describes the impact of their police work on their family and social life. The chapter also examines some of the dangers experienced by officers in the interface between their home and full time work and policing the community in which they may live.

Friendship patterns

The RUC reserve are a relatively homogeneous group, many of whom have joined the police out of a sense of duty toward community, neighbourhood and friends. It is these bonding forces that form the foundations of attitudinal formation. The support of the family is therefore seen as central to the commitment given by many reservists:

> The wife's very supportive, proud I would even say, like my own parents. Up until a few years ago I had a brother serving part time as well, unfortunately he was shot. He survived the shooting, but with work commitments, and marriage he couldn't devote as much

time so he packed it in, but that didn't alter my wife's attitude, as I say she's been very supportive. (Border reservist)

I used to come home at night and unfortunately there hasn't been a lot of change in 20 years, I used to come home from work and discuss with my wife the terrible atrocities that were happening in this country ... a couple of times my wife would say "its terrible, people are all talk and nobody seems to be doing anything", I don't think she was getting at me in particular, but things as I say haven't changed much in 20 years. (Belfast reservist)

When the wife and kids have to search round the car every time, because they use the car as much as I do, it does put a lot of pressure on you, but where we live we are used to that pressure on all the family. (Border reservist)

My mother would still say to me, especially if she hears a policeman has been shot or there is something local going on, "is it not time you were out of that, you don't need to be in that now?", but really they accept it that I am there and that its got to be done. (Belfast reservist)

In order to understand the work attitudes of the part time RUC reserve, it is important to know something about the friendship patterns that may influence their attitudes. The analysis of reported friendship patterns shows that there is little apparent contact across the community divide. It confirms data on the Northern Ireland population as a religiously isolated set of communities. Social research on Northern Ireland has found a general antipathy to cross community contact and high levels of shared religious identity between respondents, neighbours and friends. The data on the part time RUC reserve confirms this trend. Friendships are, for the most part drawn from those of the same religion:

Table 4.1
Shared religion of constable and friends

Friends of same religion	Belfast %	Border %	Country %
Most/all	77	74	72
Half/less	17	22	22
None	-	-	1
Don't know	6	5	5

Table 4.1 shows that across all three areas of location there is a strong and consistently high linkage between the religion of the part time police officer and that of the officer's friends. This is particularly true of younger constables, where over 80 per cent of those aged under 30 share the same religion of most or all of their friends. The friendships established within the community are often indistinguishable from friendships established in part time employment:

> You don't make extra friends by doing this. I mean these are usually your friends anyway that you will have known from school or church. (Border reservist)

> Well, I would say I kept my friends when I joined really, not because I joined the RUC, but because I was in here at that stage Monday, Thursday, Friday and Saturday nights and my whole social life revolved around here, so socially at first it revolved around colleagues, you came to trust them because you knew them and now you were working with them and relying on them. (Country reservist)

Within Belfast the friendship patterns at work are slightly different, officers may live outside the city and commute into their part time employment. This may lead to less stability in friendship patterns:

> Well, I have worked in a number of places ... In some of the stations up country I think there is a fantastic comradeship, it was like a family both on duty and socially, - in the city, its definitely a lot different, you have 3 or 4 maybe close colleagues but because we

work in small numbers you never really get to know people that closely. (Belfast reservist)

With working a set night one meets the people you are working with that immediate evening. We only travel in and travel out again. We live in different areas spread around the city, and being a city station no one lives within the immediate area of the station, so we are all well separated. (Belfast reservist)

There is general recognition that friendship patterns are opinion forming and reinforcing agencies, almost 70 per cent of all reservists recognized that their friendships were chosen or maintained on the basis of the sharing of agreed opinions. It is clear therefore that neighbourhood provides a main source of friendships for part time reservists. Neighbourhood is a consistently important determining factor in friendships and forms part of the pattern of shared religious identity that is demonstrated by the RUC reserve. This conforms in general to the picture of Northern Ireland provided by national research data which shows neighbourhood segregation as a major factor in attitudinal formation. Thus religion, family and friends interrelate to provide a set of meanings and range of attitudes and identities for the RUC reservist.

Full time employment

The analysis of work and leisure activity often assumes that part time work is available to those who wish to work only a limited number of hours, or are constrained to only work part time, or are required to take on additional part time hours to supplement the financial returns from full time employment. It may be that those in employment have a high degree of flexibility in their hours of full time work to enable them to manage this relationship between their two occupations. Alternatively the nature of full time employment may be such for part time police that part time employment in the reserve is viewed as dramatic compensation for the dull or routine nature of full time employment. It may also be that the dedication of a large number of hours per week to policing activity may be particularly attractive to the unemployed or those working in unstable work environments. In such a situation part time payment may provide a welcome cushion to the rigours of unemployment.

These assumptions by themselves may be simplistic. Chapter three examined the reasons for part time policing, and the financial returns available to part time officers. It is clear that part time police devote on a regular and formal basis a significant number of leisure hours to the activity of policing. There is therefore a complex relationship between the officers part time and full time employment. Any examination of the relationship between part time and full time employment needs to take account of the meanings that the reservists attach to what they regard as their work and their leisure. Similar patterns of work and leisure may therefore have differing meanings for different reservists. It is therefore necessary to examine the occupational background of reservists and the range of full time employment undertaken by them. Their financial returns and satisfactions with full time work interrelate with their part time employment, to form part of the complex structure of meanings whereby the reservist makes sense of society.

The research shows that the work of the part time RUC reserve is not a substitute for full time employment. Nearly all of male officers and over half of female officers are in full time employment. Unemployed part time police therefore represent an insignificantly small group among male reservists. Unemployed officers are almost exclusively located in the Belfast urban area. A total of 13 per cent of all male RUC reservists are self employed. The highest concentrations of self employment were in rural and border areas, and may reflect the agricultural nature of self-employment. It is a particularly male phenomenon in the RUC reserve with less than 3 per cent of female reservists being self-employed.

RUC reservists are a relatively well educated group compared to the population at large and compared with their full time colleagues. The RUC reservists would also appear to be a better educationally qualified group than the police in the rest of the United Kingdom. Parker (1982) shows that less than 18 per cent of police in Great Britain had qualifications of A Level and above; this contrasts with 30 per cent of the RUC reserve. The population of Northern Ireland contains a large percentage of educationally unqualified. Table 4.2 however shows that high proportions of the part time RUC reserve possess some form of educational qualification. Also a higher proportion of the RUC reserve than the population at large, have benefitted from higher education:

Table 4.2
Highest educational qualification
of part time officers

	Part time RUC %	Northern Ireland Population[b] %
Degree/higher eduction	17	10
A level	13	12
O level/CSE/equivalent	30	27
Other[a]	23	0
No qualifications	17	51

a   RSA, apprenticeship, etc
b   Northern Ireland census data

A study of the occupations of RUC reservists provides some indication of the social class structure of the RUC reserve. This occupational data suggests that the social class composition of the RUC reserve does not reflect the social class structure of the province. Table 4.3 suggests that the social class composition of the part time police shows a greater preponderance of white collar and skilled manual occupations, and an under representation among the semi skilled or unskilled manual occupational groupings:

Table 4.3
Occupational position of part time officers

Occupational position	RUC Male %	RUC Female %	RUC Total %	NI population* %
Professional/managerial	14	3	11	10
Other non manual	30	37	32	24
Skilled manual	40	4	30	19
Semi skilled manual	10	11	10	25
Unskilled manual	2	2	2	5
Missing/inadequate	4	44	15	7

* Northern Ireland census data

Thus not only are part time RUC reservists, for the most part in full time often skilled manual employment, but there is some evidence to suggest that these employment relationships are relatively stable. More than three quarters of male reservists and over half of female reservists have held their current full time job in excess of five years.

There is a complex social relationship between full time employment and membership of the part time RUC reserve. The nature of the social structure of the province, and occupational composition of the RUC reserve suggests that many reservists find full time employment among those from a similar social and religious background. This may indirectly serve to protect the reservist from threats within the workplace. Thus only 6 per cent of male reservists and 2 per cent of female reservists have found that their police duties have placed them under a direct threat at their full time place of work, and required them to move from their full time employment. Such changes of work that have taken place as a result of part time police activity have mainly taken place among older members of the RUC reserve:

I worked for 32 years with **** but then I was a victim of attempted assassination. I escaped with a bullet hole in my trouser leg and luckily enough my car was badly damaged so that finished me there. I'm now in the ****** trade and I've no problems there at the moment. (Border reservist)

... to cut a long story short, there were several republican elements within the firm and that led them to finding out where I lived so I left the job and where I was living in a hurry, I don't mean overnight, it wasn't that quick because the house I had been living in was mortgaged so we couldn't just up and out although it was quicker than most people, because of schemes made available through police welfare. (Belfast reservist)

There are also situations where the location of the full time employment, or the religiously mixed nature of a workforce may mean that many officers are unable to take up certain employment opportunities, or are concerned that their activities in the reserves remain unknown to many at work:

I think when some people are in this job it affects their full time employment. We have some men now who are unemployed, they go to look for jobs and once they state where that job is he just couldn't consider it and even if he resigned tomorrow he is still in association with it and it affects your whole life really. (Belfast reservist)

Where my job is I wouldn't dream of letting any of them know I have any connection with the part time security forces, and some would understand and applaud me but I would be scared in the literal sense that if any of them knew I was in the part time police I could be shot very quickly. (Belfast reservist)

It can be difficult, now I'm in the public service, that in some ways makes it easier if you need time off, there is obviously all the provisions available if your require special leave for something or time off, but you always do have suspicions about who is dealing with applications and things like that, you've seen the results of what has been carried out in the past, it does make you wonder how much you should make known to colleagues. So it has got to the stage now where I would tend to avoid contact as much as possible socially with anybody at work, simply on security grounds. (Country reservist)

There is also a general recognition that being in the RUC reserve may severely constrain the nature of the full time work in which the reservist can engage. The need to be constantly vigilant concerning personal security can cause considerable anxiety to many reservists:

73

I made plain to my employers that it doesn't affect my normal work, meaning I wouldn't leave the shop or not go somewhere because I had to go on duty, but there is pressure at the moment mentally because of some of the places you go. The current situation I know has always been bad, but in the latter months its been worse. There's some days I find it quite hard, eh, can be quite fearful. and you just have to bear it. (Border reservist)

It would hold you back from doing something different. It would be difficult for a part time reserve man if he wanted to be a postman or a milkman or a school bus driver, where he would be setting a pattern before you sent a letter to a house or a delivery man or any of those types of people. That kind of thing just wouldn't be on for a member of the security forces - not if you have a regular pattern anyway in your local area. (Country reservist)

Well, I was a milkman in ******, but only for a year, basically because it was too much of a risk. I was also in a bad area too. I'm working in a factory now so I am. (Border reservist)

Hours of work

For people to sustain part time employment it may suggest that their primary employment is relatively undemanding both in terms of hours of work and the activity associated with the post.

Table 4.4
Hours of full time work of part time officers

	All %	Male %	Female %
Under 30 hours	11	3	19
31-35 hours	7	4	10
36-40 hours	65	70	60
41-50 hours	12	17	8
Over 50 hours	5	6	3

Table 4.4, suggests however that the majority of reservists are required to work a normal 36-40 hour week. The table illustrates the disparity in work hours between men and women with almost 30 per cent of women but only 7 per cent of men working less than 35 hours in their main job.

A large proportion of male part time reservists are also required to work regular overtime in their main job. Forty eight per cent of males in full time employment were required to work overtime. A mainly male phenomenon Table 4.4, shows that of those required to work overtime, most are required to work up to 10 hours additional overtime per week on a regular basis:

Table 4.5
Hours of overtime worked
in full time employment

	Male %	Female %
Under 5 hours	45	52
6-10 hours	37	42
10-15 hours	12	4
Over 15 hours	6	-

The age distribution of those required to work overtime suggests that overtime is not a phenomenon associated with the young worker: 57 per cent of those workers required to work up to 10 hours overtime on a regular weekly basis are aged between 30 and 50 years.

A small proportion of those in full time employment are required not simply to sustain a full time job alongside their part time employment but are also required to work shift work: sixteen per cent of males and 17 per cent of females are required to work shifts. Shift working patterns mirror closely the pattern of overtime working. It is a phenomenon of middle aged workers, with 50 per cent of those required to work shifts being aged 30-50 years. Moreover it is a predominantly urban phenomenon, 70 per cent of shift workers being employed in the Belfast area.

It was thought that part time second employment would be particularly attractive to those with flexible hours of work. Such flexibility would enable the individual to make the most effective distribution of time between main and secondary employment. Part time reservists were therefore asked whether their main job left them with leisure time and provided them with flexible working hours:

Table 4.6
Flexibility of main employment

	Job leaves time for leisure %	Job has flexible hours %
Agree	34	36
Disagree	33	46
Don't know	33	18

Table 4.6 suggests that few part time police experience the flexibility and free time in their main job which would enable them to fully utilise their second job. The low availability of leisure time and flexibility in the main job is consistent irrespective of geographic location. However, it is clear that female respondents have marginally more flexibility and leisure time than their male counterparts. Forty six per cent of female part time police accept that their full time job provides them with considerable leisure time and flexibility. This compares to only 31 per cent of male part time police.

Working conditions

Part time officers were asked a series of questions concerning their employment to determine how physically and emotionally taxing they found their work. This clearly has significant implications for effectiveness in any subsequent part time employment. Table 4.7 suggests that a number of part time police find their main work extremely demanding:

Table 4.7
Physical and emotional demands of full time work

Working conditions	Always/ sometimes %	Rarely/ never %	Don't know %
Work exhausting	64	25	11
Hard and physical	39	50	11
Stressful	57	32	10

In particular 64 per cent of part time police may return from their main work exhausted before moving onto their part time policing duties, whilst a similarly high proportion find their main job stressful. Exhaustion and stress appear to be the main demands of full time employment. These conditions are not confined to a particular sex and area but are conditions experienced by a consistently high proportion of those in employment.

Few reservists appear to suffer from poor working conditions. Table 4.8, suggests that less than 30 per cent of part time officers were required on occasion to work in dangerous, unhealthy or unpleasant conditions.

Table 4.8
Working conditions in full time employment

Working conditions	Always/ sometimes %	Rarely/ never %	Don't know %
Dangerous	34	54	12
Unhealthy	23	65	12
Unpleasant	22	67	11

Where they exist, poor working conditions are more pronounced among male employees. It is also evident that those working in rural areas have a poorer working environment than those working in more predominantly urban areas.

Reservists were also asked about the security of their employment, their financial position and career prospects at work. It may be, that lack of achievement in any of these categories may assist our understanding of why the respondents obtain additional part time employment:

Table 4.9
Full time employment prospects

	Job security %	High income %	Good career %
Agree	52	14	20
Disagree	13	45	44
Don't know	35	42	36

Table 4.9 suggests that there is little positive response and a high degree of ambivalence concerning these criteria. Thus whilst most consider their job is secure, many disagree that income returns and career prospects from employment are satisfactory. Both male and female respondents share a similar distribution of opinion concerning these criteria. Similarly these views appear unaffected by location. Many reservists held the view that their full time careers had been adversely affected by their part time policing activity:

> Well, I thought last year I had a very good chance of promotion and it was between myself and another guy and I was told later that my downfall on it was because the interviewers reckoned that I did not give the same commitment to my employer as the other guy because I was involved with the part time police and I was very bitter at my employers taking that attitude because in my opinion there was no way my police work interfered with my work and I was very bitter against them. I was on the verge of appealing to my employer about it, but then I felt it would probably do me more harm than good, so, yes the part time police has kept me back from my full time job. I had to apply for permission to join the part time reserve so they are fully aware that I was involved in it. (Belfast reservist)

> I had to move in fairly short notice from one of our premises to one in a safer area because of one incident that happened. it slowed up a subsequent promotion simply because of the way things turned out,

it worried me to some degree until things changed, but I was as far away as I possibly could be. (Country reservist)

I had to turn down a promotion in my job because of a different posting in Armagh that I didn't want to touch with a barge pole because I would have got involved in trotting around the border areas, around the Blackwater River and so on. That has cost me money in the long run. (Country reservist)

It could be argued that people are attracted to a part time police career as a means of compensating for a lack of autonomy and independence within their main job. An exciting second job may also compensate for a dull and uninteresting primary employment. In reality there is little evidence to sustain this hypothesis amongst part time RUC reservists:

Table 4.10
Autonomy and independence in full time employment

	Agree %	Disagree %	Don't know %
Main job is interesting	64	8	28
Main job is independent	75	9	16
Able to plan daily work	82	18	-

Table 4.10 suggests that a high proportion of part time reservists have in reality interesting full time careers which allow a high degree of independent working. It is also clear that a considerable proportion of part time police are able to plan their daily work load maintaining a high degree of personal control over their full time employment.

It may also be argued that primary employment is failing to satisfy the income demands of respondents. The research explored the pay motivations of the respondents by examining the gross earnings part time police receive from their main job. Data was not available on average household income, however 73 per cent of respondents gave details of their gross income from their main job. There is considerable variation in average salary levels according to sex, however Table 4.11 demonstrates that the mean average salary for male part time police from their main employment is £12,130, whilst for women it is £8,200.

Table 4.11
Full time earnings of part time police

Income	Male %	Female %
Up to £7,280	14	47
£7,281-£9,360	18	29
£9,361-£11,700	21	13
£11,701-£14,500	24	6
£14,501-£40,000	23	5

The table shows that over 50 per cent of males and 70 per cent of females earn under £12,000, gross earnings from their employment, which broadly corresponds with data from the Northern Ireland population (source NI Social Survey 1989). There is a strong relationship between the social class of part time police and their full time occupation. Table 4.12 shows that 48 per cent of professional and managerial employees are in the highest income band, whilst 71 per cent of unskilled manual employees receive this lowest income from their main job:

Table 4.12
Salary and social class of part time police

	→7,280	7,281→ 9,360	9,361→ 11,700	11,701→ 14,500	14,500→ 40,000
Professional/ Managerial	7	9	14	22	48
Other non manual	22	23	17	20	18
Skilled manual	13	20	26	28	13
Semi skilled manual	40	32	17	9	2
Unskilled manual	71	15	14	-	-

There is a relationship between the size of income from the part time reservists' main job and the amount of hours the reservist is able to dedicate to part time policing. This relationship is not precise since it is mediated by other factors such as demand by the RUC for part time services. However, Table 4.13 suggests that there is an element of rational choice taking place in the amount of hours given by individuals to their part time work. Thus for example, 28 per cent of those who are in the lowest salary band from their main job also work over 10 hours per week on their part time job. This contrasts with only 16 per cent of those who are in the highest salary band who also work maximum part time hours:

Table 4.13
Part time hours and full time earnings

Full time salary band	Up to 4 hours %	4-6 hours %	6-10 hours %	Over 10 hours %
Up to £7,280	3	20	49	28
£7,281-£9,360	3	14	55	28
£9,361-£11,700	2	18	57	23
£11,701-£14,500	5	29	54	12
£14,501-£40,000	8	24	52	16

This data may go some way toward explaining why part time reservists on the border work the largest number of hours. Table 4.14, shows that part time police on the border also possess the largest number of respondents in the lower salary bands from full time employment:

Table 4.14
Full time earnings and location

Full time income	Belfast	Border	Country
Up to £7,280	18	26	23
£7,281-£9,360	19	22	20
£9,361-£11,700	20	20	18
£11,701-£14,500	23	15	18
£14,501-£40,000	20	17	21
Mean income	11,580	10,620	11,260

Few part time reservists considered that their employer was supportive of part time police work among its employees. Those that claimed that their employer was supportive often were employed in organisations with a traditional protestant recruitment base. Thus reservists were able to note:

> I don't tell anybody because it is my responsibility but working in the ******* its the sort of thing that stands for you rather than stands against you. (Belfast reservist)

> I wanted to work in ***** for a long time, and I now work in a situation where as far as my employer is concerned I think certainly they offer a lot of encouragement for anyone who wants to get involved and certainly have a positive recognition of the work being done, that's true of everyone that works here, but I know that's not always the case for lots of people. (Border reservist)

Conclusion

For many part time reservists it is clear that full time employment is a continuation of the social and religious segregation which lies at the root of Ulster society. The working environment therefore provides for these reservists a source of support and encouragement for their policing duties. Reservists recognize that they face problems when the full time employment lacks this social and religious cohesion. In these circumstances the reservist has to be circumspect about the part time employment. The workplace may be regarded as a hostile environment where the reservist confronts many of the problems that are faced in part time policing. These are not factors that translate readily to location. Thus there are many reservists who live and work in Border areas who are not self employed farmers and may be required to travel to work through potentially hostile areas, or work alongside those whom they may mistrust. Similarly the growth of public sector employment throughout the province may result in more religiously homogeneous workforces. This requires the reservist to make a series of judgements about work colleagues and about the nature of the threat which may be faced at work.

It is clear therefore that many of the economic and social assumptions that are made concerning second employment are only partially sustained. There is little evidence to suggest that the nature of full time employment facilitates secondary employment. Thus for many, the commitment to a second job is taken in the context of long hours and little flexibility in full time employment. It is also clear that full time employment provides for many respondents sufficient challenge, autonomy and control without these factors being sought in second employment. The commitment to policing as second employment may not therefore arise directly from attitudes and motives that derive from full time employment. Spare time activity forms part of a broader pattern of living, and equates more readily to the concept of "lifestyle" (see Veal 1989, Gattas 1986). This attempts to view activity in terms of the wider social order. The chapter suggests the meanings that part time police attach to their part time work derive from a network of influences. Full time employment and a range of social and leisure activities form some of the influences upon this process. Pursuits such as second employment therefore form an integral part of an overall composite view that the individual holds about the nature of society.

References

Gattas, J. (1986), Lifestyles, toward a research agenda *Loisir et Societe*, Vol. 9, pp. 529-539.

Parker, K. (1982), The educational background of the police, *Political journal*, Vol. 55, pp. 34-47.

Stringer, P. Robinson, G. (1989), *Social attitudes in Northern Ireland*, Belfast, Blackstaff press.

Veal, A. (1989), Lifestyles and status, a pluralist framework for analysis
Leisure studies, Vol. 8, pp. 141-153.

5 The attitudes of part time police reservists

Introduction

The RUC part time reserve have been in existence for over 20 years and represents a visible presence in the face of a sustained campaign of violence by the Provisional IRA. It is clear however that these 20 years have seen a number of changes in this campaign. The level of republican violence has steadily decreased. Despite the horrors of continuing atrocities the actual level of violence has decreased to the point where, as this book is being written, there has started a new and refreshing dialogue for peace. There have also been a series of political initiatives by the British government over these 20 years which have had a direct affect both upon the campaign, and also upon the sense of isolation and alienation that has been expressed by the catholic community. These initiatives have included the targeting of fair employment and job creation, and the development of an overt political dialogue with the government of the Irish Republic.

It may be that a consequence of these initiatives has been to alter and threaten the traditional certainties and beliefs of the protestant community. The levels of protestant violence have increased dramatically in recent years. The protestant political unity of the late 1960s has fragmented and divided. These changes are further compounded by increasing levels of unemployment within the protestant skilled working class. Thus many protestant communities appear embittered and increasingly alienated from the state. Reservists in many border communities describe graphically the shift of protestant population away from the border, with the consequent closure of state schools and the feelings of isolation that are held by those who remain. In Belfast, urban renewal, slum clearance and motorway development have resulted in the exodus of the populations of large areas

of the traditional protestant heartlands.   The Northern Ireland Social
Attitudes Survey (NISAS) carries out an annual examination of the manner
in which social attitudes over a range of issues have changed over a period.
there is however no detailed study of how a particular grouping within the
protestant community may be experiencing these political and social
changes.   The RUC part time reserve therefore offer a unique insight into
the current fears anxieties and concerns of an important part of the wider
protestant community.   Their views may act as a barometer of protestant
opinion and may prove critical as the province scrambles forward toward
some form of reconciliation of its divisions. This chapter therefore explores
the social identity and attitudes of part time police in the context of
Northern Irish society.   The chapter compares the attitudes of part time
reservists with those of the Northern Ireland population as a whole.   This
is achieved by comparing the social attitudes of the reservists with the data
derived from the Northern Ireland Social Attitude Survey (NISAS) which
is a regular measurement of social attitudes throughout the province.

National identity

The reservists are a relatively homogeneous group, many of whom have
joined the police out of a sense of duty toward community neighbourhood
and friends.   It is these bonding forces that form the foundations of
attitudinal formation. The research has already demonstrated that friendships
within the reserve are constructed and sustained on the basis of shared
political and religious identity.   There is also a general recognition that
friendship patterns are opinion forming and reinforcing agencies, almost 70
per cent of all reservists recognized that friendships were chosen or
maintained on the basis of the sharing of agreed opinions.

   It is also clear that neighbourhood provides a main source of friendships
for part time police. Neighbourhood is a consistently important determining
factor in friendships and forms part of the pattern of shared religious
identity that is demonstrated by the RUC reservists.   This conforms in
general to the picture of Northern Ireland provided by national research data
which shows neighbourhood segregation as a major factor in attitudinal
formation.   Religion, friendship and neighbourhood interrelate to provide
a set of meanings and range of attitudes and identities for the RUC
reservists.

   This is particularly noticeable in the context of national identity. Within
the protestant community there is considerable confusion and ambiguity

concerning its national identity. The problem is most succinctly put by Rose (1971:205) who explains that:

> The individual who deviates in his choice of identity embodies in himself the discord of society. Whereas the individual who adopts the national identification normal to his religious group has harmonized roles within his own person.

The problem confronting the reservist is that there is no single agreed national identity in Northern Ireland. In reality the label of national identity masks a range of social and political attitudes. For example the protestant who claims an Irish identity claims a subjective identification with a nationality rejected by the protestant community. It would be therefore a radical identification with a state and set of values at variance with the protestant community, and implies an embracing of the norms and values of the minority community.

Religious identity is often perceived as being under pinned by constitutional and national identities, at its simplest level therefore, protestantism becomes synonymous with unionism and identification with a sense of "British" national identity whilst catholicism becomes closely allied to an "all Ireland" national identity:

Table 5.1
National identity and religion of part time officers

Religion	British		Irish		NI/Ulster		British/ Irish		Other	
	RUC %	NI* %	RUC %	NI %	RUC %	NI %	RUC %	NI %	RUC %	NI %
Roman catholic	53	10	14	60	33	27	-	4	-	-
Protestant	75	66	2	4	16	26	6	3	1	-
None	70	55	-	12	23	22	52	2	2	-

* NISAS

Table 5.1 suggests that the almost exclusive protestant identity of the RUC reserve is reflected in perceptions of national identity. Reservists were asked to select from a list of national identities that identity which best described the way they saw themselves. The list incorporated the following national identities: British; Irish; Northern Irish; Ulster; Sometimes British sometimes Irish. An insignificant number of officers were prepared to hold an identity that incorporates in any form, the possibility of an exclusive Irish identity.

Over 70 per cent of protestant part time police see themselves as British whilst 16 per cent see themselves as having a Northern Irish or Ulster identity. The term "Ulsterman" implies a distinctive identity, one which the government attempted to foster throughout the 1950s. This failed, since the identity bore little relation to its geographic counterpart, and was also unsuccessful in attracting those in the minority community who already possessed an Irish identity. Current usage of the term would suggest a more extreme national identity which stresses the separateness of Northern Ireland from both the Republic *and* Britain. It was an expression much used by the Vanguard political movement of the early 1970s which was closely associated with constitutional plans for an independent Ulster. It implies as Nelson (1984) notes, a conception of Ulster which is "not just protestant but idealized protestant".

Catholic reservists were unlikely to see themselves as British; although over half of them did, they were much more likely than protestant respondents to see themselves as Irish or as Northern Irish/Ulster. It may be therefore that for the catholic reservist the identification with a Northern Irish or Ulster identity is identification with a compromise identity since it may recognize a separateness of identity from the Republic, whilst failing to totally embrace a British identity. It is clear therefore that for the RUC reserve as for the Northern Ireland population, national identity interacts strongly with the religious divide. However the small number of catholic members of the part time RUC reserve appear far more accommodating of a British identity and correspondingly less attracted to an Irish identity than the catholic population as a whole.

There is little general recognition of any sense of "Irishness" amongst reservists. It was asked whether reservists considered that protestants in Northern Ireland have more in common with Irish rather than British people. The research found that only 32 per cent of part time police support this proposition, and less than 30 per cent of those who subscribe to a British identity, support this thesis.

Community attitudes

The attitudes communities hold toward each other are an important barometer of social tension. Policing divided communities may require particularly sensitive antenna concerning these inter community tensions. It also requires the police to temper and be sensitive to their own background and prejudices.

The NISAS demonstrates that there is a widespread belief throughout Northern Ireland that there is religious prejudice throughout society against both protestants and catholics:

Table 5.2
Religious affiliation of part time officers and perceptions of prejudice

	P/T RC %	NI* RC %	P/T Prot %	NI Prot %	P/T None %	NI None %
Prejudice against catholics:						
Lot	33	38	20	27	23	39
Little	60	46	53	36	55	42
Hardly any	7	11	25	30	18	15
Prejudice against protestants:						
Lot	-	15	40	27	29	31
Little	33	40	27	42	41	43
Hardly any	47	31	10	24	25	20

* NISAS
Table ignores not known category

It is clear from Table 5.2 that members of the RUC reserve share the belief that there is considerable prejudice in society, directed at both communities. As a group, part time police do not differ in any major way from the Northern Ireland population but it is clear that protestants, who make up the majority of part time reservists, tend to think that there is more prejudice against protestants in Northern Ireland than against catholics. Similarly catholic members of the RUC reserve were considerably more receptive to the view that there is prejudice against catholics, than the idea of prejudice against protestants. The views of the RUC reserve appear as an exaggerated reflection of the views of the protestant and catholic communities in Northern Ireland.

Table 5.3
Location of part time officers and perceptions of prejudice

	Belfast %	Border %	Country %
Prejudice against catholics:			
Lot	24	10	17
Little	48	49	45
Hardly any	21	28	27
Prejudice against protestants:			
Lot	36	50	30
Little	40	32	44
Hardly any	12	6	11

Table ignores not known category

These views vary according to location. Reservists who work in border stations hold stronger views than their colleagues in other areas. Half of the border reservists believe that there is a lot of prejudice against protestants. Similarly border reservists are less willing to accept the notion of a lot of prejudice against catholics:

... There is probably more bitterness now. Its different now, sometimes they cannot employ you if your a protestant. Its not that they don't want to, its just that they may not be allowed to by law, but if you were a catholic ...

You just have to watch and that's it and say damn all at the end of it. We're the ones that are seen on the TV as the villains ... they'd be nice to you one minute and shoot you the next. There was a buddy there blown up about Magherafelt or some place and the boy that blew him up, many a time halved his lunch with him but you never hear the likes of that on the TV. (Border reservist)

In addition to their views on the current state of community relations, the police were also asked their views concerning future relationships between the two communities. Perceptions of the future of community relations are intertwined with views about the future of the state and the political processes that are taking place to resolve these issues:

Table 5.4
Location of part time officers
and community relations

	Belfast %	Border %	Country %
Relations with catholics getting:			
Better	50	44	46
Same	37	42	42
Worse	11	11	5
Relations with protestants getting:			
Better	8	5	8
Same	43	39	42
Worse	45	54	44

Table 5.4 shows a concern by members of the reserve at a perceived increase in hostility toward the protestant community. Over half of all the part time police believe that there is now less prejudice against the catholic community than there was five years ago, whilst almost half of protestant part time police believe that there is now more prejudice against their own community. The table shows that this developing feeling of prejudice against protestants is held particularly strongly among those working in the border areas.

This may in part reflect a growing sense of isolation among reservists working on the border. This sense of isolation may be accentuated by continuing "troubles" and political marginalisation as Dublin and Westminster draw closer together on the problems of Northern Ireland. It results in relations between the two communities being highly prescribed and limited to the non contentious, politically neutral:

> ... I would say where I live, more or less in a nationalist area, and I have a farm right round me, they are mainly roman catholics, a few policemen or UDR, but the rest of them are roman catholic. But I farm among them and say the cattle broke out into my land, they all would get together and help you out. But then there's that wee thing in your mind, I suppose its just because I'm in the security forces and some of my brothers too, I mean, you could stand and have a conversation about the weather or the cattle, but that's about it. Its always on safe territory. I keep them on the safe side, I mean, some may say, that's terrible what happened that fellah was shot the other night, but I always say very little, but he'd be testing you to see if he could find out your attitude. I would always play it "cool" because I know they are only testing my reaction. (Border reservist)

Political progress and dialogue between two relatively polarized communities, implies the recognition of some degree of commonality of interests. It implies some common denominator from which more sophisticated dialogue may develop. A number of questions were therefore asked which explored among part time police the possibilities of such a commonality of interests existing between the two communities. Reservists were asked in particular, whether they think that catholics in Northern Ireland have more in common with Northern Irish protestants than they have with catholics in the Republic. The question implies the possibility of the existence of an identity which crosses the religious divide. It suggests that catholics may subsume a general Irish nationalist identity within a shared Northern Irish commonality. It is essentially a liberal collectivist view of the state deriving its stance from perceptions of a commonality of catholic and protestant opinion:

Table 5.5
Part time officers and a commonality of interests

Commonality of interests	RUC All %	RUC RC %	RUC Prot %	RUC No religion %
Agree	48	73	42	57
Disagree	25	7	22	27
Don't know	27	20	34	16

Table 5.5 suggests that there is some support for the proposition. Overall 48 per cent of part time reservists accept that there is a commonality of interest between communities. However this figure masks a considerable divergence along religious lines with over 70 per cent of catholics accepting the proposition compared to only 42 per cent of protestant respondents. This may confirm the view that the process of joining the reserves for a catholic recruit may require that recruit to absorb a set of values and attitudes that may contrast strongly with those views held by the catholic community. It may also suggest that those recruited from the catholic community appear more liberal and tolerant of opposing views than many others within the force.

There appears to be little optimism among the reserves for a long term reduction in the importance of religion in relations between the communities:

Table 5.6
Part time officers and the future
of religious demarcation

Will religion always have an affect on relations	RUC RC %	RUC Prot %	RUC No religion %
Yes	73	79	79
No	13	10	11
Don't know relations?	14	11	10

The overwhelming majority of members of the RUC reserve, irrespective of religious identity, accept that religion will remain a major line of demarcation between communities in Northern Ireland for the foreseeable future. The view may be summed up in these quotes:

> You cannot escape it, you are what you are, and they're them. Its like that, different schools, different pubs, different churches, and a different flag. You'll never get any of them to stand up for the Anthem ... (Belfast reservist)

> Well I think it (religion) is important, certainly in our family. I mean, look at other countries where they have lost it. The country is ruined ... we've got to keep our faith. (Country reservist)

> Down here we're fighting over land. protestant farms being under threat, the only son being killed. That'll not stop, that will go on as long as there is a Border to protect. (Border reservist)

It is perhaps therefore unremarkable that members of the RUC reserve hold strong views concerning their attitudes to the policing of the Border with the Irish republic. Members of the reserve who work on the Border are undecided about the need to increase cooperation with the security forces in the Republic in order to police the Border. It is those reservists in the city and country who regard increased cooperation as the way forward in the policing of the Border:

Table 5.7
Part time officers and
increased cooperation with the Republic

Increased cooperation	Belfast %	Border %	Country %
Agree	55	40	51
Disagree	29	44	26
Don't know	16	16	23

Social issues

The schooling of children in Northern Ireland directly reflects the social and political configurations that have been described. Schools divide into "controlled" schools which are state financed and predominantly protestant in both pupils and teachers, and "maintained" schools which are almost exclusively catholic and financed in part by the catholic church. In recent years considerable political and financial support has been given by the government to a developing "integrated" sector of education.

Social research confirms that there is considerable and growing support for integrated education with over 60 per cent of the population in favour of government support of integrated education. The NISAS shows a greater proportion of catholics (67 per cent) in Northern Ireland than protestants (58 per cent) advocate a policy of integrated education. The views of the RUC reserve generally conform to this pattern of opinion:

Table 5.8
Part time officers and attitudes to schooling

Schools as cause of division	Belfast %	Border %	Country %
Agree	72	49	56
Disagree	20	36	30
Don't know	8	15	14

This table, shows that there is general support amongst part time police for the proposition that separate schooling is a major cause of division in society. Protestant members of the RUC reserve are far less supportive of this proposition than their catholic counterparts, 80 per cent of whom recognize the division that separate schooling causes in society. The table shows that the distinction of views are particularly pronounced on a regional basis, less than 50 per cent of part time police who work in border stations subscribe to the notion that separate schooling causes division in society, this contrasts to over 70 per cent of part time urban based police who do subscribe to this notion. Members of the RUC reserve who work in the Belfast and country areas are more supportive of integrated education:

> ... Well, we seem to be staying at the same point all the time. Its a policy of containment. I joined and thought in a few years the country would be as good for my kids as it was for me then, and it is frustrating that when they are now 18 or 19 years old they can't run around as they want. In fact one's gone off to England, and good luck to her, they are better off out of this country I feel. That's not the way I felt 17 or 18 years ago, I felt we would make things right. We need to start in the schools we should get people being taught together. I strongly believe that's where are problems start. (Belfast reservist)

It is within the border areas where attitudes appear stronger. For many, integrated education is state education with only the hostility of the catholic church standing in the path of full use of the state system:

... Its sadness in that I cannot see any solution to the trouble and I have said this more times than enough to my family and colleagues. We are bought up in different schools, different clubs, and that's where the problems start. If all the children started off at the same school they would all learn what is right and wrong. (Border reservist)

... It's not about education at all, that's a side issue, look, if you want to put it into religion, most of the people I mix with are all protestant and all stick to protestant pubs and don't mix at all. You can't go into a roman catholic pub - you would be asked to leave, we are segregated that way, but its not of your choice, its really a fact of life. You wouldn't feel safe and before the night would be out you would possibly be picked on anyway. What they would say is "what the hell is he doing in here anyway", so its your choice. Well, really you never think, "I'll not go into a roman catholic pub, I'll go into a protestant pub", you just automatically go to your local where you can sit and relax and have a decent drink. You never think in your mind its a protestant pub or a roman catholic pub. That's what life here is all about. Education wouldn't change anything because the catholic church would want to keep control over its side. That way it can keep it all going ... you know, pushing to do away with the border and all that. (Border reservist)

On other social matters the part time police as a sub group of the Northern Ireland population are less willing than the population at large, to allow dissent and protest to be organized against government:

Table 5.9
Part time officers and attitudes to
protest against government

	All RUC %	RUC RC %	RUC Prot %	RUC No Relig %
Agree	47	67	42	68
Disagree	19	20	29	18
Don't know	34	13	29	14

Catholic members of the RUC reserve have a generally more liberal attitude than their protestant counterparts. Almost 70 per cent of catholic members of the reserve argue that the population should be allowed to organize and protest against government.

There is considerable ambivalence amongst members of the RUC reserve on issues relating to general income distribution and welfare. Social Research has found that there is considerable support throughout the Northern Ireland population for the view that the gap between rich and poor is too great. Part time police are generally equally divided about whether there is great inequality of income:

Table 5.10
Part time officers and attitudes to equality

"One law for rich, one for poor"	All RUC %	RUC RC %	RUC Prot %	RUC No relig %
Agree	40	47	35	36
Disagree	25	27	31	32
Don't know	34	27	30	32

It is the protestant reservists who remain the more conservative grouping on this and other social issues. Thus whereas almost 50 per cent of catholic reservists believe that income inequality has an impact in society, this view is not shared by their protestant colleagues. There is a similar ambivalence amongst members of the reserve concerning their attitudes to social security. Thus whereas 60 per cent of catholic members of the reserve consider those in receipt of social security are deserving members of society, their protestant colleagues again remain a more cautious grouping. The table suggests that protestant reservists are undecided about whether social security recipients are in genuine need:

Table 5.11
Part time officers and attitude to social security

"Social security is exploited"	All RUC %	RUC RC %	RUC Prot %	RUC No relig %
Agree	38	33	65	30
Disagree	33	60	30	41
Don't know	29	7	34	29

Law and order

Previous surveys of attitudes in the province have noted that on law and order issues there are often considerable differences of opinion between protestant and catholic members of Northern Ireland society. Issues of law and order are of central concern to all police. It may therefore be expected that the police hold clear, unambiguous and agreed views concerning these issues.

Central to the issues of law and order and the control of terrorism is the use by the state of internment. This is a procedure that has been used on a number of occasions since the establishment of the state. Internment removes into custody those whom the police believe are perpetuating the terrorist campaign. It also relieves the state of the burden of establishing guilt before a court. It is therefore a highly controversial method of bypassing court processes since the police are not required to obtain conviction. Internment found widespread support among the part time members of the RUC reserve:

> ... If they can do internment once or twice then they can do it two or three hundred times, yes, and rid the place of them on both sides. I mean, at the start there was only IRA, but then UDA; and all the branches started off, INLA and every time they are all in it for what they can get out of it, and none of them want this trouble to stop because there's big money involved in it. (Belfast reservist)

We should go after the people not sit and stand until they do something and then react to that. Every night you are briefed, you know who they are, you know they're going to operate in the town. I believe those people should be interned. (Border reservist)

... Well, it might be alright because apparently the authorities know that, a good few of these boys and can't do anything about it, if there was internment they could do it then, but otherwise they can't touch them. (Country reservist)

This research shows that whereas protestant part time officers generally reflect protestant opinion in Northern Ireland on these issues the views of catholic part time officers often contrast vividly with those of the catholic population at large. The most interesting illustration of this divergence is on the vexed issue of capital punishment.

Social research on this issues demonstrates perhaps surprisingly that the views of the Northern Ireland population are more liberal on the issue of capital punishment than those of the rest of the United Kingdom. Only 59 per cent of the Northern Irish population support the use of capital punishment in contrast to 74 per cent of the rest of the United Kingdom. However in Northern Ireland views on the death penalty differ dramatically according to religion with only 31 per cent of catholics supporting the use of the death penalty compared to 77 per cent of protestants. The table below outlines the views of the RUC reserves:

Table 5.12
Part time officers and attitudes to the death penalty

"For some crimes the death penalty is most appropriate sentence"	All RUC	RUC RC	RUC Prot	RUC No Relig	All NI	All GB
	%	%	%	%	%	%
Agree	85	60	79	86	59	74
Disagree	9	20	7	11	41	23
Don't know	6	20	14	3	-	3

Table 5.12 demonstrates that among part time reservists there is a high level of support for the return of capital punishment in Northern Ireland, with 85 per cent agreeing that it is the most appropriate form of punishment for some crimes. Catholic part time police are far more supportive of the death penalty than the catholic community at large with 60 per cent supporting the proposition. Support for capital punishment also varies with area with over 90 per cent of part time police who work along the border, supporting the death penalty:

> ... I think they want to make a tougher attitude to terrorists, he is too well supported and protected and its so easy for them to go across the border where you can't get at them, so easy for them to disappear. They want to use the SAS far more to go into Donegal and bring them out. At the moment they are serving a few years for murder and then coming out and crossing the border to plan their next one. We are fighting with one hand tied, if there was hanging, this thing would have quietened down years ago. (Border reservist)

> ... I think at the minute the government is quite happy with the situation as it is, as long as it doesn't effect them. Soldiers were killed yesterday, and about 10 people killed in the last four days, but that doesn't make any difference, there's been things that have happened, like Enniskillen and nothing, as everyone thought could happen worse than that. After Enniskillen they could have bought in capital punishment and no one would have objected, all they would have said was that it was 20 years too late. (Border reservist)

Similarly support for a stronger sentencing policy is felt particularly strongly among those part time police who work on the border. These police demonstrate in general, a more authoritarian range of attitudes on law and order issues. On the matter of sentencing policy over 90 per cent of border reservists believe the sentencing policy of the courts is too lenient, this attitude is often coupled with a feeling that the Westminster government is less committed to defeat of terrorism than (by implication) a unionist government in Northern Ireland would have been:

> ... Nothings' going to change according to the government policy, its not going to end anyway. This government doesn't care. The younger people must see there's not much satisfac-

tion in joining because in the old B Specials in the farming community, when a young lad became 18 years of age he couldn't wait to get joining, but now we've been let down by the government so much, no ones' interested. There is no will on the government's behalf to do something constructive. (Border reservist)

... Its certainly not the fault of the police, we need stronger courts to hand out bigger sentences. We are the pawns and here to do what we are told, government, yes, I do think its their fault, they could have done an awful lot more. They are standing and they are still standing doing nothing, but a crisis erupted in the Falklands, or a war broke out in the Middle East and we see it all happening, everyone into action, the governments' ready to up stakes and employ millions into it, if she had've done the same thing here and backed us and the forces here, I think the troubles would have been contained an awful lot easier. (Border reservist)

The operation of a democratic system of law and order implies a general consent and adherence to the law throughout society. The NISAS identified a high proportion of the population who considered that it was legitimate not to obey a law that was considered wrong. It may be expected that the police should be much stronger upholders of the law than the population at large. Table 5.13 shows that this is not directly the case:

Table 5.13
Part time officers and attitudes toward the law

"Law should be obeyed even if wrong"	All NI %	NI RC %	NI Prot %	All RUC %	RUC RC %	RUC Prot %
Agree	38	28	48	56	67	52
Disagree	36	48	25	17	33	14
Don't know	26	14	27	27	10	34

Only 52 per cent of protestant part time members of the RUC believe that the law should be obeyed even if it is considered wrong. This broadly equates with the response of the Northern Irish protestant population. There is however, a marked contrast between the views of the catholic population at large and that of its part time police. Table 5.13 shows that a considerably higher proportion of catholic part time police (67 per cent) than the catholic population as a whole (28 per cent) argue that law should be obeyed. Indeed support for the law appears far higher among catholic members of the RUC reserve than among their protestant colleagues.

This dissenting protestant tradition has become focused upon the issue of the Anglo-Irish Agreement. This Agreement establishes for the first time a direct influence for the government of the Irish Republic on matters concerning Northern Ireland. The Agreement therefore strikes at the roots of unionism, and may symbolize the increasing sense of protestant isolation from government:

> If they had been a bit harder way back in the 1970's it may have been over by now. I haven't heard much about this conference (Anglo-Irish Conference) but I read in the paper and they say that they would fight terrorism to the very last, by Jesus, they're not fighting it in Northern Ireland. They've been saying that for 20 years. They'll fight it till the last drop of Ulster blood, yeah, it'll be Ulster blood. (Border reservist)

> ... Show me one good thing that has come out of this Anglo-Irish Agreement. Of course I am opposed to it. It hasn't stopped the killing. All its done is to open the door for the IRA so they can say just one more shove. (Belfast reservist)

> ... It doesn't make any difference one way or the other, as far as I see, there were people being killed before (the Agreement) and still people killed after. It hasn't made the changes it was supposed to make. We hear stories about the co operation, but if anything its made it worse. Before the Agreement we used to talk direct now everybody has to go to the top to pass the intelligence over and pass it down again, rather than the two sergeants either side of the border speaking direct to each other. (Border reservist)

> ... I think now there's very little direct conversation from station to station. We used to operate out of ******** and used to be very good and literally chat across the bridge, (the

103

border) but I don't think that necessarily goes on any more. (Border reservist)

... Well if you ask me as an ordinary person, yes I would say I am against it (the Agreement), I think its a sellout by the British government, not that it surprises me! But if you ask me as a policeman, I would say whats' changed? (Country reservist)

It is this fear of a betrayal and a sense of a lack of government commitment toward the defeat of terrorism that is at the root of many of the views on law and order held by older members of the reserves. It is these attitudes that may determine the position adopted by the protestant community on any likely end to hostilities and resolution of the conflict. Older reservists, and in particular those who live and work along the border, regard the campaign in simplistic terms of win lose and defeat. Thus the troubles come to an end when the Provisional IRA is defeated or surrenders its weapons and manpower. There is a more elusive, more moderate view held by some reservists, a younger grouping in the relatively safer country areas and parts of the city. This more moderate view recognizes the language of compromise and negotiation that may be inherent in any end to the present campaign.

These are the extremes of opinion that strike at the heart of the current dilemma for government. Thus the very process of formally ending violence by the Provisional IRA may require the government to reconcile these two unionist positions:

... I think this could go on and on and on for a good lot of years yet and in a sense it could go on forever. I don't think they want to stop it actually ... The authorities, the government, I don't think they want to stop this at all. There's no real desire on the part of the British government to win this war. If they do get them, like the two boys and the women the other night they got four years and they'll be out in two and be at it again. If they were put in for 40 years or something like that it would be better, it would be a better job so it would. If they are talking about life or 20 years, it should be life not letting them out in five years or whatever. (Belfast reservist)

... I think the British government is afraid of world opinion, like the SDLP here say if you harass the catholic population too much you'll drive them into the Sein Fein and IRA but how are you going to deal with the IRA unless you do harass them! You kept thinking every time something big happened, like the time there was 18 soldiers killed and they said they would definitely do something about it and when Mountbatten was killed that day, but they didn't do anything. Yet they could do it. Take for instance eight soldiers killed within a fortnight, they had three men dead. And indeed, selective internment you know, there's a very useful weapon that everyone seems scared of. (Border reservist)

... I feel very strongly, if anything happens to me I'm just another statistic, end of story, the government won't want to know, the police won't want to know and the only people that would miss me would be my kids and family and a few friends and after a while that will die away and my like will have been lost for no cause and I firmly believe that and noone will convince me otherwise,you see whether we are winning or not winning, we are not even trying to win. (Border reservist)

You take how many thousand deaths from both sides, and over twenty years of fighting, and for what? ... no you've got to be prepared to talk to these people, you've got to be prepared to find out why ... (Belfast reservist)

Conclusion

This chapter has explored the range of social attitudes held by part time police. Previous chapters have suggested that the part time police are a predominantly protestant force. There is a small minority of catholic members of the force. These members may have been in the part time RUC reserve for some time since there is little evidence of any recent upsurge of catholic recruitment to the force. The religious composition of the part time RUC is reinforced by the friendship patterns and neighbourhoods from which the part time RUC recruit. This confirms the typical phenomenon of the province as having religiously isolate community and friendship patterns.

The chapter shows that views of the protestant members of the part time RUC often exist as an exaggerated reflection of the views of the wider protestant community. Views on a number of social issues are held more strongly than the community at large. Similarly within the force there are marked contrasts in views according to factors such as religion age and

105

location. Thus those part time police who work on the border often hold stronger views than their colleagues in Belfast. Similarly catholic members of the force have a range of views that may often contrast with the catholic population. This is particularly notable on issues of national identity and issues of law and order. Catholic members of the part time RUC often appear to be more in tune with the views of the part time force as a whole than with the catholic community. However on social issues catholic members appear to hold more liberal views than their protestant colleagues with much stronger support for integrated education and the right to protest against government.

6 Toward a typology of reservist behaviour

Introduction

This book has set out to demonstrate that the meanings part time members of the RUC reserve attach to their membership of the RUC are located within their experience of work, friendships and the wider community in which they live. The book has explored a number of issues concerning the nature of part time policing in Northern Ireland and the attitudes of reservists. It has examined the historic development of the RUC reserve organisation, the nature of part time policing, and the work and social influences that affect the part time officer. It has attempted to indicate answers through description of the social and work context of the reservists and description of their attitudes toward Northern Ireland society.

This book therefore provides a unique sociological portrait of part time police officers. The major perspective which guided the investigation, and was instrumental in defining the limits of the research, was social action. The utility of the perspective is that it suggests that the study of groups such as the part time RUC reserve can be approached primarily in terms of the meanings that part time reservists attach to their membership. Such an approach enables the RUC reserve, its purpose and direction at any one time, to be seen as a function of social action and thus subject to interpretation and reinterpretation.

The study gives practical illustration to a developing body of literature which recognizes the importance of studying behaviour in organisations in terms of configurations of values, ideals and norms which the community invests in the organisation. It is an approach which recognizes that people are continually constructing and reconstructing their social world through their interactions (Benson 1977). Voluntary involvement in the policing of

Northern Ireland can therefore be seen as deriving from these experiences of everyday life. This study has focused directly upon the community as the starting point for the study of the RUC reserve. It demonstrates that study of an organisation from the viewpoint of the meanings members of the community attach to the organisation can provide insight into both organisation and community. It also demonstrates that the activities of people in organisations are not mechanistic, simple processes but are the result of various interpretations of a community's past, its histories and cultures. The study argues for an analysis of the police in terms of the historical processes which gave rise to it so that the potential for particular social groups within the organisation becomes visible.

The social action approach of this study is perhaps most relevant in the context of a society constrained by strict ethnic divisions. The study suggests that the rigidity of norms and the lack of deviance within the protestant community and the nature of the threat that society faces, have produced a particular type of part time policing that can be best understood in terms of a mix of quantitative and qualitative analysis. The research provides a case study of meanings that some members of the protestant community attach to a range of social issues. In addition, it has provided an empirical base for the development of a typology of the organisation's membership that offers insight into the protestant community itself.

The chapters provide critical evidence to support this thesis. Chapter two suggests an interrelationship between the state and its reserve police which suggests an interdependence of the old B Specials with the community from which it developed and drew its support. The chapter suggests that throughout the years of unionist control of the political processes in Northern Ireland the reserve police in the form of the B Specials provide a general and continuing support for the values of unionism. The reform of the RUC that followed the Cameron Report and the riots of 1969, removed the B Specials and established a new RUC reserve. It is a process which enabled the new members of the newly established part time RUC reserve either to re enforce the traditional explanations and behaviour that many imported from their membership of the B Specials, or to seek a movement toward modernity and a more rational calculative mode of activity.

Contemporary data which confirms this central theme about the meanings of membership of the part time reserve is contained within the next three chapters. These chapters have explored the attitudes toward part time policing, the full time employment and values of reservists in three distinct geographical areas of Northern Ireland. The identities of the areas and their social and religious composition serve as foundations for the social attitudes and behaviours held by reservists who live and work in these areas.

It is clear from the research that considerable variations exist in the background and meanings that part time police attach to their work. Different work settings produce different sets of beliefs, values and attitudes. These tend to characterize different groups of people who work in the same occupation. This is the dynamic of occupational culture which means that it varies between groups and between work location. The general findings of this research show that there is a series of conflicts within the RUC reserve between tradition and modernity. There are many who hold a strongly dichotomous view of society which explains behaviour by reference back to past events. They are strongly British with a long tradition of service. These part time police view society as structured along dichotomous religious lines of national identity. Border respondents stand out as an example of this type of part time police. Within the border area the part time police maintain much closer friendship patterns with each other than in other areas. Part time officers on the border have a much stronger attachment to their church and to their neighbourhood than police in other areas. A consequence is that border respondents hold much stronger views than their Belfast or country colleagues.

In marked contrast there is a more elusive and numerically much smaller group. This group seeks to minimize the scale and threat of inter community conflict and is more receptive to the idea of increased cross community contact, and less influenced by traditional values. Examples of this type of part time police may be found among younger members, many of whom appear less receptive to the influences of church and neighbourhood than their older colleagues. Similarly examples may exist in the country area where attitudes and values appear less extreme than those held by many of those part time police who work along the border.

In a number of notable respects, catholic part time police officers differ markedly in their views not simply from their protestant colleagues but also from the catholic population at large. In many ways catholic respondents fit more closely to the younger more radical members of the force. The research provides evidence to show that catholic members of the part time RUC when joining the force have to detach themselves more fully from the views of the catholic community than their protestant work colleagues. The process of joining the force may therefore prove a far more difficult process for catholic than protestant recruits.

The reservist comes into contact with sets of ideas and values within a particular social milieu from which is constructed a meaning system to explain membership. Within the context of Northern Ireland, it is necessary to develop a typology of the RUC reservists which recognizes that its protestantism and unionism that remain at the root of social meaning, but is also sensitive to the differing perceptions of social identity and minority relationships held within the protestant monolith.

The typology

The research has categorized RUC reservists according to work location. This has proved a useful vehicle for identifying differences concerning attitudes to work and views of reservists. It is however a limiting structural analysis. It tells the reader little about differences in orientation toward policing that may be influenced by religion, age or sex. It offers no explanation of those attitudes which may transcend regional location. It also offers little assistance to the reader in examining the problems of change within the society and its impact upon policing. It is therefore possible to construct a more sophisticated typology of members of the RUC reserve. It is through the use of a typology that connections can be made between social action and differing meaning systems. Through these type constructs it is possible to pose questions
about the nature of the organisation and its future.

The typology of membership of the RUC reserve which is outlined here relates fundamentally to the range of social attitudes and behaviours that compose the meaning systems of our actors. The categories that are developed are, of course, all ideal types, developed so as to highlight certain characteristics among reservists. Since they are ideal types that are necessarily abstractions from reality, but they are empirically derived from the range of characteristics revealed by this research. It is therefore a typology which possesses both qualitative and quantitative foundations. It is unlikely that any reservist fits exactly one of the types, but members of the reserve can be said to approximate to one or other of the types outlined:

Liberal

Warrior ———————————————————————— **Worker**

Conservative

It must be remembered when considering this typology that the protestant community imposes upon its membership a range of internalized rules and sanctions against their breach. Thus variations of behaviour and attitude are, of necessity, often merely slight shifts of emphasis rather than dramatic clashes of attitude and behaviour. Most RUC reservists could be said to roughly approximate to one type or another in the sense that each may fit most of the characteristics of a particular type. The aim of the typology is not to produce any exact model of membership, but rather to aid the impression and understanding we can gain of the RUC reserve. It highlights important areas of difference between the membership.

The warrior

The type constructs of this research relate back to Webers (1964) classic sociology. Weber distinguishes between zweckrational and wertrational categories of social action. The wertrational is identified as an orientation based upon traditional sets of absolute values about the nature of society and the role of institutions within it. Much literature in the field of socialization provides a ready explanation for the development of traditional values. In the context of the RUC reserve this we may be referred to as the *warrior* type.

This type subscribes to a set of values that place heavy reliance upon group solidarity and the pursuit of public esteem which may be associated with the task of defeating terrorism. This type places a high value upon informal group cohesion, loyalty and a sense of comradeship. The warrior type holds a sense of fraternity which may be associated with a station or area. The warriors in this study may therefore place a high value on friendships derived and sustained through their police commitment. They would have a high level of satisfaction from the tasks of policing. It may also be expected that commitment of the warrior to the RUC reserve may either be primarily based upon a sense of public duty, and a conscious commitment to the police contribution to the solution of social and political problems; or on a more traditional view of policing in Northern Ireland, whereby part time policing is viewed as contributing to maintaining a power structure. This is a power structure which sees the catholic community in a supplicant role in a unionist society.

The mutually contradictory groupings within society result in actors within the protestant community displaying a high degree of loyalty to the power structure and to disavow any consideration of the minority view. Thus the warrior sees membership of the RUC reserve primarily in terms of a dichotomous vision of society and the need to defend protestant values against the minority community. Membership of the RUC reserve is seen as an ostensible expression of this defence. This type of ideological perspective structures the adherent's views and provides a source of values

111

with which the warrior explains the RUC reserve and its membership. It is a meaning system that explains behaviour by reference back to past events, a type of behaviour that reflects a past era when the RUC, residing within protestant community, developed a mutual interdependency and reinforcement with a government, drawn from the same community.

This type of member of the reserve is more prevalent within the border areas of our research. Here the geographical location places the reservist in a situation where any dissent within the protestant community and its institutions would be seen as directly threatening to the protestant community. This may suggest that the greater the degree of community segregation, the more important such ideological factors became in structuring the ideas of the community. The warrior may view the policing tasks of the reserve primarily as a means of protecting a protestant way of life, and thus may seek to enter the ranks of the reservists because of the critical function policing may hold in the protestant community. The warrior may be most prevalent among reservists exposed to evangelical and strict presbyterian influences, supporting a fundamentalist theology; that is, a type of protestantism which see catholicism as heresy. On the issue of national identity there can be no accommodation with a view that recognizes the possibility of a non protestant influence. The warrior views him/herself as British, and political behaviour reflects such an ideology. There is clearly no possibility by the warrior type for any political allegiance which implies a weakening or possible removal of a unionist identity.

The worker

The zweckrational category of social action identified by Weber implies a purely rational calculative orientation, it is a rejection of traditionalism, and is often associated with the modern Instrumentality thesis of Goldthorpe (1968). This may be referred to as the *worker* type. This type stands in marked contrast to the warrior in possessing a primary instrumental, rational calculative orientation to the work. Part time policing is seen simply as a job, offering a particular set of terms and conditions of employment and a particular authority structure. The job of policing is not seen as possessing any particular moral connotations, thus the worker underplays the importance of loyalty, morale and "esprit de corps" as aspects of the organisations' culture which may be valued highly by the warrior. In the context of this study, workers may place a high value on the financial returns to the part time work. There may be different concern with the political context of policing in an internal security situation to that held by

112

the warrior. The worker may regard the tasks inherent in such policing as a police requirement to "hold the ring" for all the parties to settle their differences. This may contrast with the more assertive stance of the warrior who may have a more direct concern with the outcome of any possible negotiations. The worker may have a more direct concern with the financial returns associated with part time policing and more recognition of the part that the part time reserve plays in the general employment context in Northern Ireland. The organisation may offer financial security. It may offer the opportunity to move into full time policing. It may also offer a measure of job security in an economically uncertain environment. The part time reserve provides for a number of officers, both status and an element of financial security. It may also provide a vital compensation for the lack of opportunity or status, offered in the full time job of the part time officer. Thus there may be particular concern with the satisfaction of a variety of personal needs.

The warrior/worker dichotomy may be intersected by political allegiance. The research may add to the understanding of Ulster protestantism which Elliot (1981) suggests has suffered from being viewed as a monolithic unit. Edwards (1970) distinguished a two fold typology of Ulster protestantism: the "confident" for which the minority community does not feature in its frame of reference, and the "fearful" who are hyperconscious of the minority presence. This typology is similar to Rose's (1971) who talks of protestant "locals" and "cosmopolitans". Both these distinctive types have good points of similarity with the warrior. All view the minority community as monolithic, and hostile to Ulster protestantism. All develop an ideological perspective which provides a source of values which gives legitimacy to the protestant cause. Wright (1973) identifies the liberal unionist who seeks to accommodate the minority community and to minimize their scale and threat. The liberal unionist is developed in contrast to other fundamentalist types. The liberal unionist has few points in common here with most warriors. Wright's analysis is on the basis of political activism.

These analyses of protestantism are on the basis of differing perceptions of catholicism which are central to all divisions of protestant life. The most helpful distinction is that of Wright's (1973) distinction between conservative and liberal unionists. This in varying ways has been picked up by McKitterick in 1980 and Nelson in 1984. Thus the warrior/worker typology may be inter relate closely to a conservative/liberal dichotomy.

This liberal worker therefore stands in contrast to the conservative warrior. The latter essentially rejects the minority community, whereas the liberal worker holds an essentially liberal unionist position, that it is possible to achieve minority support for unionism. The liberal worker is unlikely to be found in the border area but forms a significant minority of our respondents in other locations. It is an Ulster loyalist perspective, therefore, which specifically bypasses the religious divisions which the conservative warrior embraces. The liberal worker member of the reserves represents the remnants of an O'Neill tradition. The liberal worker is decreasingly influenced by the roles of church and state. Mainly Church of Ireland or liberal presbyterian, the mid road member is more responsive to the possible separate development of protestant institutions. Thus, the RUC reserve is not seen as primarily or necessarily intertwined with the protestant power structures which the liberal worker accepts have altered significantly in the post Stormont era. This type of reservist still perceives identity as British, although there may be acceptance of an Ulster identity, since the liberal worker may be concerned to defend Ulster against inclusion into the Republic. The liberal worker would share with the conservative warrior an upbringing and leisure pattern that reflects a lack of contact with the catholic community.

The typology may be illustrated in terms of the position of these types on a number of key issues:

Issue	Warrior	Worker
Powers of the reserve	Too Restrictive	About right
Future of reserve	Limited future	Optimistic
Satisfaction with reserve	Satisfied with job	May find limits frustrating
Family background in RUC	Strong	Weak
Anglo/Irish dialogue	No support	Conditional support
Integrated education	Limited support	Strong support
Sentencing Policy	Too lenient	Satisfactory
Inter community contact	None	Highly prescribed
Capital punishment	Support	Support

Meanings derive from the reservists' experiences of everyday life within the community. Organisations like the part time reserve therefore can be seen as strongly affected by these experiences. The typology can be illustrated by the way particular views of reality become dominant and reflected in the organisation, and the role of these ideas and values in buttressing the structure and affecting the success and direction of change.

The future

It is in the realm of change in the organisation that the behaviour of reservists and their relationship to this typology is most readily illustrated.

The attitudinal position routine and life style of part time officers are the formative influences upon the manner in which their police work is perceived. These warrior and worker attitudes function therefore as an operational code which is used by reservists in their police work. Punch (1985) suggests that such an operational code is used by police to manage the interface between themselves and society.

Many of the studies of police occupational culture have been undertaken in the context of understanding deviant behaviour within the organisation (see Barker 1977, Barker and Roebuck 1973, Chatterton 1975). Occupational culture is an elaborate way of dealing with problems confronted by work and developing a social justification for the work. Bryant (1974) notes therefore that occupational culture also defines social conformity, it provides reason and explanation for certain kinds of behaviour. The development of a typology of policing therefore helps to locate deviance as part of that organisational arena where people hold differing rationales.

Warrior attitudes may therefore be seen as deviant, they are myth systems that may initiate support and sustain certain kinds of behaviour. It is a series of attitudes that helps the officer define behaviour toward the clientele. Warriors may be viewed as deviant since they undermine the drive by the RUC to broaden its acceptability to the catholic community. It is a situation where the powerful culture of a work group runs counter to that of the organisation. It may be that the process of part time policing operating as it does, often at the interface of two hostile communities serves to reinforce warrior attitudes. Barker (1977) argues that the tasks of policing may offer an opportunity structure for deviance, a socialization structure for deviance, and group reinforcement. Warriors may therefore possess a range of attitudes that run counter to the need to increase catholic recruitment into the force. They are also a range of attitudes that may be perceived as fundamentally hostile to that community whose support is most sought by the RUC.

The RUC reserve is therefore subject to the traumatic process of organisational change. Mintzberg (1987) has shown that in studies of organisational change there exist a number of constraining conditions caused by the technological, bureaucratic and social momentum existing within organisations. Adaptation of the RUC to these changes in its environment are both constrained and conditioned by these forces. This research also suggests that contexts can be interpreted differently among actors, thus change within the RUC is a power process in which dimensions such as culture and ideology become central.

The typology may assist understanding of the processes associated with change within the RUC reserve. This change may be illustrated by the model outlined below:

A model of change in the part time RUC

CONTENT

Objectives
and assumptions
of change

PROCESS ——————————————————— CONTEXT

Change managers
Formulation/Implementation

External   **Internal**
Economic   Resources
Political   Capability
Social   C u l t u r e

Content

Banton (1970) suggests that the reasons for change within the police, arise from a need to police those whose support for the police appears to be weakest. This as at the root of much of the debate concerning community policing. The objective of the change process for the RUC reserve may therefore be summarized as making the reserve more acceptable to the community at large and the minority catholic population in particular. This may be seen as continuing the process noted by Brewer (1991) of moving the RUC from a traditionalist model of policing toward a professionalism and uniformity of standards implied within the more legal rational approach.

Part time policing offers a unique bridge between the full time force and the community. It poses particular challenges in the context of Northern Ireland. Thus any consideration of change within the part time reserve needs to recognize that this part time force provides a unique opportunity for members of the community to register their opposition to terrorism. A part time force provides an alternative focus to the more extreme avenues of political action that may be available to members of the community. It has been long recognized however by the RUC that there are a number of attendant problems in the operation of a large part time volunteer force alongside the full time police. The part time police lack integration into the full time organisation. Their numbers and geographic location reinforce a predominantly loyalist image and ensure a surfeit of numbers in those geographic areas where part time services may be required least.

Context

A process of political and social change may cause anxiety from within the majority protestant community. This community which has traditionally seen the RUC as "its" police, may view with concern any change in the structure or training of the reserves. Central to the context of change is the dramatic increase since 1990 in protestant loyalist violence. From 1992 loyalist violence has outstripped violence from the Provisional IRA and has become a major concern to the security forces.

There are a number of possible social, economic, and political factors which may go some way toward accounting for this increase in protestant violence. There has been a dramatic decline in the strength of the Belfast protestant community. Since 1976 the size of the protestant population of Belfast has almost halved. Slum clearance and urban development led in the 1960s and 1970s to the growth of new towns outside Belfast, the growth of Antrim town, Craigavon and the dormitory areas of Bangor and Newtownabbey. The movement of protestants out of the city, and away from their traditional community locations has resulted in the attendant social problems of new estates, increased isolation and the inevitable decline in community pride and loyalty that was traditionally associated with the protestant areas of Belfast. This decline has occurred against a backcloth of apparent catholic community renewal and regeneration.

There has also been a significant economic decline in the province. This decline has affected the traditional industries of Belfast which gave the protestant working class its sense of industrial identity and pride. Belfast grew and prospered on shipbuilding and engineering. Industries that provided the economic backbone to an assertive and powerful protestant working class. Since the 1970s shipbuilding employment has fallen dramatically from 12,000 to under 3,000 employees, with similar losses in the engineering industries. This has had a fundamental impact upon protestant economic power.

This social and economic decline has occurred alongside a number of political changes. The protestant community has experienced a continuing decline in its political institutions and erosion of its political power. The removal of the unionist government has been followed by the reduction in powers of local government and a developing political dialogue with the Republic. Increased cooperation and political dialogue between the Irish Republic and the government of the United Kingdom may lead to increased fears of unionist isolation in the bargaining process. It may also be that increased dialogue at what ever level may be perceived as suggesting a degree of success to the forces of violent republicanism.

These events have resulted in a retreat that is seen as cultural, political and economic. The protestant community may therefore see itself as alienated and marginalized from developments in the province. It may contrast itself with a catholic community that appears cohesive, disciplined and politically successful. It is this fear of increasing marginalization that sustains the conditions for protestant paramilitary violence.

In such a situation of increased protestant violence, the traditional relationship between the police and the protestant community is placed under direct threat. Such change may play directly upon those fears implicit in the attitudes of those warriors identified within the typology. It may in some situations make the position of the part time officer untenable as the threat against the police shifts to a threat from within their own community. This has been experienced in recent years by a number of full time and part time officers, and resulted in a number of attacks:

> We did have to move house, owing to, well, a direct threat, so we moved house ... they wanted to move us within a week but we just felt well, we had built our house and we just couldn't afford to move and thought right we will try and stick this out so eventually then we did give in and did move out. I think its difficult to keep it from people that you are in an organisation because you are out and about and once one person knows its for sure that other people are going to get to hear about it. (Country reservist)

> Being in the reserve has caused me to move house twice. Basically, the first time, the wife was getting a lot of phone calls whenever I was on duty, asking where I was, no names mentioned, just where was I. That was in 1978, I think, the

119

phone would ring, and someone would say "your husband's just left the police station, but will he make it home ?" As I got into the house the phone would ring "you made it" and that lasted about a week and I was gone, I moved to XXXXXXXX then and then I came across someone observing my movements there, no matter what time I came home off duty he would be out putting his milk bottles out and there was pressure there too, so we moved again. (Belfast reservist)

It is also clear from the research that the small number of catholic members of the reserves possess a range of attitudes that stand in marked contrast to the wider catholic community. Membership of the RUC reserves therefore appears a much more difficult process for the catholic recruit who when joining, has to become more fully detached from his own community than does the protestant recruit. The occupational culture of the reserves may ensure that catholic recruitment is limited to those who are prepared to subscribe to a set of values often apparently irreconcilable with those of the catholic community at large. The part time catholic recruit also often faces the additional problem of living and working within a community, elements of which may directly oppose membership of the RUC.

The research confirms the reserves' membership as a religiously and socially isolate group. It conforms in general to the picture of Northern Ireland provided by national research data which shows residential segregation as a major factor in attitudinal formation. This may provide serious questions for the recruiting agenda for the RUC. The RUC is subject to the imperative to broaden its recruitment base to make it more reflective of society at large. The research has shown that the major source of recruitment is the neighbourhood in which they live and their friendships. The research also shows neighbourhood and friendships to be religiously homogeneous. The consequence of this is that the RUC reserve is in danger of recruiting "much of the same, from the same", with the same religious composition and attitudes replicating themselves through the recruitment process. The evidence of this research shows that the attitudes of reservists are to some degree, tempered by location and service. Such a socializing process however, offers no direct challenge to the distorted nature of the RUC reserves' recruitment.

Process

It is clear that the attitudes and purpose of the part time reserve needs to be given careful consideration by the RUC. It may represent an element of the force that has not appeared susceptible to the processes of change and developing professionalism that have been identified within the wider force. Part time members of the force may be in a unique position. As part time workers, their identification with the prevailing full time occupational culture may well be lessened by the shorter time during which they are exposed to it, and by their possession of another occupational role. The process of establishing shared values and beliefs in their police work between themselves and their full time colleagues is undermined by their limited involvement within the organisation. Also as part time officers they may not work within an established work group and may remain relatively isolate from the mainstream of police activity. This feeling of marginality was often reflected in attitudes of reservists toward the wider organization:

> ... I tried to see if they would assist me to get my phone number changed (after a series of anonymous threats) but they said nothing could be done. There are a number of people who I have met in my travels who have been equally very upset at the way the organisation has helped or hasn't helped them in a moment of crisis like that. (Country reservist)

> We pay into the Police Federation which is the police union, we pay in every month and yet they don't want to know us. As long as the regulars are happy, it doesn't matter about us. They would promise you the world to beat these terrorists, the night my house was bombed but the next day the promises meant nothing. (Belfast reservist)

> I was going home and I noticed a car behind me that was following me ... The first thing I did was take the registration number and rang the duty inspector and informed them, but they didn't take me seriously ... I firmly believe the part time reserve are more at risk that the regular force It would be nice I suppose to come into work and have 10 or 12 armed men around you that are on your side ..." (Border reservist)

There is absolutely no man managing skills in our rank structure, there is a lot of brass, silly men running about who haven't a clue who have never been on the street, who have never dealt with the public and all he can say to you is "your boots aren't shined up, come to my office, I want to see you". Until that's sorted out the force will never be effective. They're not interested in the part time, just so long as we are there. (Belfast reservist)

Failure to reform may leave the reserves vulnerable to disbandment. It is already clear that there is little recruitment of reservists along the border areas of the province. This is primarily because of the difficulties inherent in protecting these members of the reserve. It is possible that any political settlement that increases the influence of the Irish Republic, may lead to increasing hostility toward the RUC from within the protestant community. In such an event the most politically attractive organisational option may be to disband an unreformed, marginal aspect of the police resources.

A study of the more senior reservists who work along the border suggests they conform closely with a model of conservative warrior behaviour. An older grouping than the rest of the reservists, they are located firmly within the traditional orthodoxies of the protestant community. The research suggests that on almost any scale they reflect a high degree of certainty and absoluteness of conviction concerning the nature of society and its institutions. There is moreover incidental evidence to suggest that many who are active within the reserve have similar patterns of activity within other protestant organisations. It may be that the nature of this activism throughout the community may serve to legitimate authority among the wider reservist constituency. These reservists by virtue of their status and involvement in the wider community and their advocacy of conservative, warrior beliefs may be in a powerful gate keeping position in respect of their capacity to control the debate and sets of values inherent in the organisation. They may act as a major brake to any change process and offer a challenge to any reform option.

Conclusion

Berger (1967) suggests that it is the ability of certain actors to create and sustain power enough to enforce their interpretations of the organisation and its environment that determines the direction and strategy of the organisation. Thus within the part time RUC reserve, the ability of the RUC to change dominant rationalities is primarily determined by their ability to make their interpretation of what the organisation should be, legitimate with reservists, thereby creating support or acquiescence in the organisation. The focus may therefore need to be at the level of recruit training. Mannen and Katz (1979) argue that it is recruit training that forms a vital part of the process of culture indoctrination. It offers the opportunity to engineer social change with a captive group. The current recruit training of two weeks for part time reservists may do little to address the clash between warrior attitudes and the need for a more professional part time reserve. Training should focus more directly on the attitudes and values associated with worker reservists outlined in the typology. This is a group more receptive to change more anxious to identify cross community contact and who view the reserves as playing a role in supporting the wider political arena, rather than identified with any specific political agenda. This is a group that relates more directly to those professional members of the full time force who regard their role in terms of objective single standards of conduct, and who empowered both formally and informally to identify the objectives and direction of the organisation and its role within the community at large.

References

Banton, M. (1970), Social order and the police, *Advancement of science journal*, September, pp. 48-57.

Barker, T. (1977), *Peer group support for police Occupational deviance*, British journal of criminology, Vol. 15, no. 3, pp. 353-367.

Barker, T. Roebuck, J. (1973), *An empirical typology of police corruption: a study in organisational deviance*, New York.

Berger, P. Luckmann, T. (1967), *The social construction of reality*, Penguin.

Benson, J. (1977), Organisations a dialectical view, *Administrative science quarterly*, Vol. 22, pp. 1-21.

Bryant, C. (1974), *Deviant behaviour: occupational and organisational bases*, McNally, Chicago.

Chatterton, M. (1975), *Organisational relationships and processes in police work*, Phd, University of Manchester.

Chesshyre, R. *The force: inside the police,* Date and Pub NK.

Edwards, O. (1970), *The sins of our fathers. The roots of conflict in Northern Ireland*, Gill and Macmillan.

Elliot, R. and Hickie, J. (1971) *Ulster: a case study in conflict*, Longman.

Mannen, J. Katz, R. (1979), Police perceptions of their work environment, *Sociology of work and occupations journal*, Vol. 6, No. 1, pp. 31-58.

McKitterick, D. (1980), *The class structure of unionism*, Vol. 4, pp. 28-33, Crane Bag.

Nelson, S. (1984), *Ulster's uncertain defenders: loyalists and the Northern Ireland Conflict*, Appletree Press.

Punch, M. (1985), *Conduct unbecoming the social construction of police deviance and control*, Tavistock.

Rose, R. (1971), *Governing without consensus*, Faber and Faber.

Vick, C. (1982), Ideological responses to riots: *Police journal*, Vol. 55, pp. 262-278.

Appendix

1   Age.
Please tick appropriate box.

Under 20	☐₁
21-24	☐₂
25-29	☐₃
30-34	☐₄
35-39	☐₅
40-44	☐₆
45-49	☐₇
50-54	☐₈
55+	☐₉

2   Sex.

Male	☐₁
Female	☐₂

Please continue …

3   Marital status.

Married	☐1
Single	☐2
Widowed	☐3
Separated	☐4
Divorced	☐5

4   **Married respondents only**

Does your spouse work, on either a full time or part time basis?

Works part time	☐1
Works full time	☐2
Does not work	☐3

If yes, please indicate your spouse's full job title:

_____

5   **All married respondents**

Please indicate the number of dependent children in your household? (A dependent child is one aged under 16 years - or aged under 19 if in full time education.)

No children	☐0
One	☐1
Two	☐2
Three	☐3
Four	☐4
Five	☐5
Does not work	☐6

Please continue ...

6   From the list below, please place a tick in the box against the *highest* qualification you possess.

Higher degree (specify _____) ☐ 01

First degree (specify _____) ☐ 02

Graduate membership of a professional institute

(specify _____) ☐ 03

BTEC/BEC(Higher)/TEC(Higher)/HNC/HND ☐ 04

Teaching qualification ☐ 05

Nursing qualification ☐ 06

A levels or equivalent ☐ 07

BTEC or BEC (National/General)TEC(National/General ONC/OND) ☐ 08

O levels or Equivalent ☐ 09

City and Guilds ☐ 10

Recognised trade apprenticeship completed ☐ 11

Other qualification (specify _____) ☐ 12

Please continue …

THIS SECTION CONCERNS INFORMATION COVERING THE TIME WHEN YOU ARE NOT UNDERTAKING POLICE DUTIES

7   Are you currently in full time employment (ie over 30 hours per week) or part time employment (ie less than 30 hours per week)?

	Full time	Part time
Yes	☐₁	☐₁
No	☐₂	☐₂

If yes to Question 7 are you an employee or self employed?

Employee	☐₁
Self employed	☐₂

If no to Question 7 are you:

Housewife	☐₁
Retired	☐₂
Unemployed	☐₃
Student	☐₄
Other, specify _____	☐₅

All retired/unemployed

8   What was your main job title in your last job?

_____

Please continue ...

Unemployed Only

9   How long have you been unemployed?

                                                              Years Months
                                                              _____

IF YOU ARE RETIRED GO DIRECT TO QUESTION 25

IF YOU ARE UNEMPLOYED GO DIRECT TO QUESTION 25

IF YOU ARE EMPLOYED GO DIRECT TO QUESTION 12

Self employed only

10   Do you employ any other people?

                                    1-5 employees   ☐1

                                    6-24 employees   ☐2

                                    25+ employees   ☐3

                                    No employees   ☐4

Please describe briefly what you mainly do in your job.

_____

_____

11   How long have you been self employed?

                                    Under 3 months   ☐1

                                    3-6 months   ☐2

                                    6 months but less than 1 year   ☐3

                                    1 year but less than 2 years   ☐4

                                    2 years but less than 5 years   ☐5

                                    5 years but less than 10 years   ☐6

                                    10 years but less than 20 years   ☐7

                                    20 years or more   ☐8

                                                         Please continue .

129

Employees only

12   What is your main job title? _____

13   Please describe briefly what you mainly do in your job _____

_____

_____

14   Do you have managerial or supervisory responsibilities?

Manager ☐1

Foreman/supervisor ☐2

Not manager or supervisor ☐3

15   How long have you been continuously employed by your current employer?

Under 3 months ☐1

3-6 months ☐2

6 months but less than 1 year ☐3

1 year but less than 2 years ☐4

2 years but less than 5 years ☐5

5 years but less than 10 years ☐6

10 years but less than 20 years ☐7

20 years or more ☐8

Please continue ...

16   How many employees are there at your place of work?

Under 25	☐1
25-50	☐2
51-100	☐3
101-200	☐4
201-300	☐5
301-400	☐6
401-500	☐7
Over 500	☐8

17   How many hours a week do you usually work in your main job?
(excluding paid or unpaid overtime)

Enter number of hours   _____

18   Are you required to work paid overtime?

Regularly	☐1
Occasionally	☐2
Never	☐3

19   How many hours of paid overtime do you usually work in a week?

Enter number of hours   _____

20   Are you required to work shift work?

Yes	☐1
No	☐2

Please continue ...

131

All employees and self employed

21 What are your average **gross** earnings (ie before all tax and deductions) from your **main** job? (excluding paid overtime)

£_____

21a And what period does this cover?

a week ☐1

a month ☐2

a year ☐3

22 In your main job, how often …

		Always	Often	Sometimes	Hardly ever	Never	Don't know
i)	… do you come home from work exhausted?	☐1	☐2	☐3	☐4	☐5	☐6
ii)	… do you have to do hard physical work?	☐1	☐2	☐3	☐4	☐5	☐6
iii)	… do you find your work stressful?	☐1	☐2	☐3	☐4	☐5	☐6
iv)	… are you bored at work?	☐1	☐2	☐3	☐4	☐5	☐6
v)	… do you work in dangerous conditions?	☐1	☐2	☐3	☐4	☐5	☐6
vi)	… do you work in unhealthy conditions?	☐1	☐2	☐3	☐4	☐5	☐6
vii)	… do you work in physically unpleasant conditions?	☐1	☐2	☐3	☐4	☐5	☐6

Please continue …

23   Which of the following statements about your main job is **most** true?

Please tick one box only

My job allows me to design or plan **most** of my daily work. □₁

My job allows me to design or plan **part** of my daily work. □₂

My job **does not really** allow me to design or plan my daily work. □₃

24   For each of these statements about your **main** job, please tick one box to show how much you agree or disagree that it applies **to your job**.

Please tick one box on each line.

		Strongly agree	Agree	Neither agree nor disagree	Disagree	Strongly disagree	Don't know
i)	My job is secure.	□₁	□₂	□₃	□₄	□₅	□₆
ii)	My income is high.	□₁	□₂	□₃	□₄	□₅	□₆
iii)	My opportunities for advancement are high.	□₁	□₂	□₃	□₄	□₅	□₆
iv)	My job leaves a lot of leisure time.	□₁	□₂	□₃	□₄	□₅	□₆
v)	My job is interesting.	□₁	□₂	□₃	□₄	□₅	□₆
vi)	I can work independently.	□₁	□₂	□₃	□₄	□₅	□₆
vii)	In my job I can help other people.	□₁	□₂	□₃	□₄	□₅	□₆
viii)	My job is useful to society.	□₁	□₂	□₃	□₄	□₅	□₆
vii)	My job has flexible working hours.	□₁	□₂	□₃	□₄	□₅	□₆

Please continue ...

25   Have you ever worked in full time employment outside Northern Ireland?

Yes ☐₁

No ☐₂

Please continue ...

134

THIS SECTION IS MAINLY CONCERNED WITH YOUR PART TIME WORK WITH THE RUC

26   How long have you been a member of the P/T RUC?

Under 1 year	☐₁
1-2 years	☐₂
2-3 years	☐₃
3-4 years	☐₄
4-5 years	☐₅
5-10 years	☐₆
10-15 years	☐₇
Over 15 years	☐₈

27   Have you ever worked part time in any of the services listed below? (If you have worked part time for more than one of the services, please indicate the service *immediately prior* to joining the RUC.)

UDR	☐₁
Fire service	☐₂
TAVR	☐₃
None (proceed to Q29)	☐₄
Other, specify _____	☐₅

28   What were the principal reasons for your leaving that part time employment?

_____

_____

29   What was/is your father's main occupation?

Jobtitle_____

Please continue ...

135

30   Please outline below what your father did/does in his main occupation?

_____

_____

_____

31   Has your father ever undertaken part time police duties?
      (eg including the USC)

                                    Yes   ☐1

                                    No   ☐2

                                    Don't know   ☐3

32   Have any of your brothers or sisters ever undertaken part time or regular RUC police duties?

                    P/T RUC   F/T RUC

      Yes   ☐1   Yes   ☐1

      No   ☐2   No   ☐2

      Not applicable ☐3   Not applicable   ☐3

Please continue ...

136

33   What is your average **gross** monthly income from part time work with the RUC?

Under £80	☐1
£81-90	☐2
£91-100	☐3
£101-110	☐4
£111-120	☐5
£121-130	☐6
£131-140	☐7
£141-160	☐8
£161-180	☐9
£181-200	☐10
£201-220	☐11
£221-240	☐12
£241-260	☐13
Over £261	☐14

34   How many hours *per week* on average would you devote to your P/T RUC employment?

Under 2 hours	☐1
2-4 hours	☐2
4-5 hours	☐3
5-6 hours	☐4
6-8 hours	☐5
8-10 hours	☐6
Over 10 hours	☐7

Please continue ...

35 Generally speaking, in what activity would you spend most of your P/T RUC employment? (Please tick one answer only)

Guard duties ☐1

Mobile patrolling ☐2

Desk reception activity ☐3

Beat patrolling ☐4

Other, specify _____ ☐5

36 Please rank 1-5 the principal duties of the P/T RUC in order of your preference?

Guard duties ☐1

Mobile patrolling ☐2

Desk reception activity ☐3

Beat patrolling ☐4

Other, specify _____ ☐5

37 Do you think the tasks the P/T RUC are required to undertake are too restricting, too wide or about right?

Too wide ☐1

Just right ☐2

Too restricting ☐3

38 On how many occasions have you been required to change your place of duty since becoming a member of the P/T RUC?

Once ☐1

Twice ☐2

Over three times ☐3

Never ☐4

Please continue ...

39   Have you ever been required to change your place of full time employment because of your part time RUC work?

Yes ☐1

No ☐2

Not applicable ☐3

40   How did you first hear about the P/T RUC?

Advertisements ☐1

Work colleagues ☐2

Neighbours ☐3

Family ☐4

Other, specify _____ ☐5

41   The colleagues you work with on the P/T RUC, would you call them:

Close friends ☐1

Friends ☐2

Work acquaintances ☐3

42   Have you ever considered applying for the full time RUC?

Yes ☐1

No ☐2

Please continue ...

43   Here are some reasons people give for joining the RUC part time - could you **rank them 1-5** in order of importance:

Interest and variety of work ☐1

Pay ☐2

Good companionship ☐3

Pleasant working conditions ☐4

A sense of performing a public service ☐5

44   During your time in the P/T RUC, have you ever made an arrest?

Yes ☐1

No ☐2

Don't know ☐3

45   During your time in the P/T RUC have you ever assisted in an arrest?

Yes ☐1

No ☐2

Don't know ☐3

46   In the next five years do you think the role of the P/T RUC will increase or diminish in importance?

Increase ☐1

Stay the same ☐2

Diminish ☐3

Please continue ...

140

47   How satisfied are you with your work in the P/T RUC?

Very satisfied $\square_1$

Fairly satisfied $\square_2$

Neither satisfied or dissatisfied $\square_3$

Fairly dissatisfied $\square_4$

Very dissatisfied $\square_5$

Please continue …

141

48   How influential do you think the Police Federation is for the part time RUC in the following areas:

		Extremely influential	Very Influential	Marginally Influential	Not Influential	Not known
i)	Securing higher pay	☐1	☐2	☐3	☐4	☐5
ii)	Securing satisfactory working conditions	☐1	☐2	☐3	☐4	☐5
iii)	Communicating a good public image of the RUC	☐1	☐2	☐3	☐4	☐5
iv)	The communication of information and views within the RUC	☐1	☐2	☐3	☐4	☐5
v)	In influencing legislation in the interests of police	☐1	☐2	☐3	☐4	☐5
vi)	In the provision of welfare benefits	☐1	☐2	☐3	☐4	☐5
vii)	In fostering the efficiency of the RUC	☐1	☐2	☐3	☐4	☐5
viii)	In helping on questions of disciplinary charges	☐1	☐2	☐3	☐4	☐5
ix)	In fostering good relations between the regular and P/T RUC	☐1	☐2	☐3	☐4	☐5

Please continue ...

142

49   Do you consider that the Federation should be more or less militant than at present in its approach to negotiations?

More militant ☐1

Satisfactory ☐2

Less militant ☐3

Not known ☐4

50   Have you ever required the Federation to take up an issue on your behalf?

Yes ☐1

No ☐2

Don't know ☐3

51   Have you ever required the Operational Liaison and Welfare Committee to take up an issue on your behalf?

Yes ☐1

No ☐2

Don't know ☐3

THIS SECTION IS MAINLY CONCERNED TO EXPLORE ATTITUDES TO A NUMBER OF SOCIAL ISSUES RELEVANT TO NORTHERN IRELAND

52   From where would most of your friendships come?

P/T RUC ☐1

F/T employment ☐2

Neighbourhood ☐3

Church ☐4

Other, specify _____ ☐5

53   Would you say your friends generally share the same opinions on issues as yourself?

Yes ☐1

No ☐2

Don't know ☐3

54   About how many of your **friends** would you say are the same religion as you?

All ☐1

Most ☐2

Half ☐3

Less than half ☐4

None ☐5

Don't know ☐6

Please continue ...

55   How many of your **neighbours** are the same religion as you?

All	☐1
Most	☐2
Half	☐3
Less than half	☐4
None	☐5
Don't know	☐6

56   Which of these **best** describes the way you usually think of yourself?

British	☐1
Irish	☐2
Ulster	☐3
Northern Irish	☐4
Sometimes British, sometimes Irish	☐5
Other, specify _____	☐6

Please continue ...

57   Do you regard yourself as belonging to any particular religion?
      If yes, which?

No religion	☐1
Christian - no denomination	☐2
Roman Catholic	☐3
Church of Ireland/Anglican	☐4
Baptist	☐5
Methodist	☐6
Presbyterian	☐7
Free Presbyterian	☐8
Brethren	☐9
Other Protestant, specify _____	☐10
Other, specify _____	☐11
Refused to say	☐12

58   How often nowadays do you attend your place of worship?

Once a week or more	☐1
At least once in two weeks	☐2
At least once a month	☐3
At least twice a year	☐4
At least once a year	☐5
Less often	☐6
Never	☐7
Varies too much to say	☐8
Refused to answer	☐9

Please continue ...

146

59   Below are a number of statements, would you please tick the box that most closely represents your views about each of these statements.

		Agree	Disagree	Don't know
i)	Catholics in Northern Ireland have more in common with Northern Ireland protestants than with catholics in Republic.	☐1	☐2	☐3
ii)	Northern Ireland protestants have more in common with Irish people than with British people.	☐1	☐2	☐3
iii)	Separate roman catholic and protestant schools have been a major cause of division in Northern Ireland.	☐1	☐2	☐3
iv)	There should be increased co-operation on all levels across the border with people in the Republic.	☐1	☐2	☐3

60   Do you think there is **a lot, a little or hardly** any prejudice against protestants in Northern Ireland nowadays?

A lot   ☐1

A little   ☐2

Hardly any   ☐3

Don't know   ☐4

Please continue ...

147

61   Do you think there is generally **more, less or about the same** religious prejudice against protestants now than there was five years ago?

More now ☐1

Less now ☐2

About the same ☐3

Other, specify _____ ☐4

62   Do you think there is **a lot, a little, or hardly any** prejudice against catholics in Northern Ireland nowadays?

A lot ☐1

A little ☐2

Hardly any ☐3

Don't know ☐4

63   Do you think there is generally **more, less or about the same** religious prejudice against catholics now than there was five years ago?

More now ☐1

Less now ☐2

About the same ☐3

Other, specify _____ ☐4

64   Do you think that religion will **always** make a difference to the way people feel about each other in Northern Ireland?

Yes ☐1

No ☐2

Don't know ☐3

Other, specify _____ ☐4

Please continue ...

148

65   Please tick one box for each statement below to show how much you agree or disagree with it.

		Strongly agree	Agree	Neither agree nor disagree	Disagree	Strongly disagree	Don't know
i)	There is one law for the rich and one for the poor	☐1	☐2	☐3	☐4	☐5	☐6
ii)	Young people today don't have enough respect for traditional values	☐1	☐2	☐3	☐4	☐5	☐6
iii)	People who break the law should be given stiffer sentences	☐1	☐2	☐3	☐4	☐5	☐6
iv)	People should be allowed to organise public meetings to protest against the government	☐1	☐2	☐3	☐4	☐5	☐6
v)	For some crimes, the death penalty is the most appropriate sentence	☐1	☐2	☐3	☐4	☐5	☐6
vi)	Schools should teach children to obey authority	☐1	☐2	☐3	☐4	☐5	☐6
vii)	The law should always be obeyed, even if a particular law is wrong	☐1	☐2	☐3	☐4	☐5	☐6
viii)	Censorship of film and magazines is necessary to uphold moral standards	☐1	☐2	☐3	☐4	☐5	☐6
vii)	Many people who get social security don't really deserve any help	☐1	☐2	☐3	☐4	☐5	☐6

149

Bibliography

Albeda, W. (1977), Changing industrial relations in the Netherlands, *Industrial relations*, Vol. 16, pp. 1-14.

Banton, M. (1970), Social order and the police, *Advancement of science journal*, September, pp. 48-57.

Barker, T. (1977), *Peer group support for police occupational deviance British journal of criminology*, Vol. 15, no. 3, pp. 353-367.

Barker, T. Roebuck, J. (1973), *An empirical typology of police corruption: a study in organisational deviance*, New York.

Berger, P. Luckmann, T. (1967) *The social construction of reality*, Penguin.

Benson, J. (1977), Organisations a fialectical view, *Administrative science quarterly*, Vol. 22, pp. 1-21.

Bent, A. (1974), *The Politics of law reform*, Lexington.

Bessinger, G. (1981), Israeli police in transition, *Police studies*, Summer, pp. 3-8

Brewer, J. (1988), *Police public order and the state*, Macmillan.

Brewer, J. and Magee, K. (1991), *Inside the RUC*, OUP.

Broderick, (1974), see Reiner the politics of the police.

Bryant, C. (1974), *Deviant behaviour: occupational and organisational bases*, McNally, Chicago.

Cain, M. (1973), *Society and the policeman's role*, Routledge, Kegan, and Paul.

Cameron Commission, (1969), *Disturbances in Northern Ireland*, Cmnd. 532, Belfast HMSO.

Chatterton, M. (1975), *Organisational relationships and processes in police work* Phd, University of Manchester.

Chesshyre, R. *The force: Inside the police*, Date and Pub NK.

Dachler, M. and Wilpert, B. (1978), Conceptual dimensions and boundaries of participation in organisations, *Administrative science quarterly,* Vol. 23, pp. 1-39.

Edwards, O. (1970), *The sins of our fathers. The roots of conflict in Northern Ireland*, Gill and Macmillan.

Elliot, R. and Hickie, J. (1971), *Ulster: a case study in conflict*, Longman.

Farrell, P. (1971), *Ireland's English question*, Batsford.

Gattas, J. (1986), Lifestyles, toward a research agenda, *Loisir et Societe*, Vol. 9, pp. 529-539.

Goldthorpe, J. (1973), A revolution in sociology? *Sociology*, Vol. 7, pp. 449-462.

Goudsblom, J. (1967), *Dutch society*, New York.

Gurvitch, M. (1971), The image of the police in Israel, *Law and society review,* Vol. 5, pp. 367-387.

Hezlet, B. (1972), *Fermanagh B Specials*, London, Tom Stacey.

Holdaway, S. (1983), *Inside the British police - a force at work*, Blackwell.

Hunt Committee, (1969), *Report of the advisory committee on police in Northern Ireland*, Cmnd. 535, Belfast HMSO.

Knijt, J. (1959), *Influences of denominationalism*, Archives de sociologie des religions iv, No. 8, pp. 105-111.

Leon, (1989), The Mythical history of the special, *Liverpool law review*, Vol. xi, (2), pp. 187-197.

Lorwin, V. (1971), Segmented pluralism, Ideological cleavages and political cohesion in smaller European democracies, *Comparative politics*, Vol. 3, pp. 141-175.

Mannen, J. Katz, R. (1979), Police perceptions of their work environment, *Sociology of work and occupations journal*, Vol. 6, No. 1, pp. 31-58.

McKitterick, D. (1980), *The class structure of unionism*, Vol. 4, pp. 28-33, Crane Bag.

Manning, P. and Butler, A. (1982), Perceptions of police authority, *Police journal*, Vol. 55, 82. pp. 333-344.

Nelson, S. (1984), *Ulster's uncertain defenders: loyalists and the Northern Ireland conflict*, Appletree Press.

Oliver, J. (1978), *Working at Stormont*, Institute of public administration.

Parker, K. (1982), The educational background of the police, *Political Journal*, Vol. 55, pp. 34-47.

Police advisory board for England and Wales, (1981), *Second working party on the special constabulary* .

Punch, M. (1985), *Conduct unbecoming the social construction of police deviance and control*, Tavistock.

Reiner, R. (1978), *The blue coated worker*, Cambridge university press.

Reiner, R. (1982), Who are the police? *Political quarterly*, Vol. 53:2, pp. 165-180.

Reiner, R. (1985), *The politics of the police*, Wheatsheaf books.

Reiser, G. Israeli police politics and profiles, *Police studies*, Vol. 6, No. 1, pp. 27-35.

Rose, R. (1971), *Governing without consensus*, Faber and Faber.

Scarman tribunal, (1969), *Report of the tribunal of inquiry into violence and civil disturbances in Northern ireland*, Vol. 1, and 2, Cmnd. 566, Belfast HMSO.

Stringer, P. Robinson, G. (1989), *Social Attitudes in Northern Ireland*, Belfast, Blackstaff Press.

Thompson, J. (1967), *Organisations in Action*, New York, McGraw Hill.

Tierney, M. (1978), *Modern Ireland*, Gill and Macmillan.

Tonnies, F. (1971), *Community and society*, OUP.

Veal, A. (1989), Lifestyles and status, a pluralist framework for analysis, *Leisure Studies*, Vol. 8, pp. 141-153.

Vick, C. (1982), Ideological responses to riots: *Police journal*, Vol. 55, pp. 262-278.

Windmuller, B. (1969), *Labour relations in the Netherlands*, Attica.

Weber, M. (1974), *The theory of social and economic organisation*, Oxford university press.